RECOVERING
IN RECOVERY

− the actuality of _recovering_ in recovery.

memory
pg 8

SHELBY JOHN, LCSW-C

For Ryan, Grace, Nora and Derek
Nothing worth doing is easy.

INTRO

I N EVERY LIFE THERE IS A BEFORE AND AN AFTER. A disaster, success or loss that defines how you were before and then what it was like after. Marking off periods of time like inches on a growth chart at the pediatrician's office, you go on. If you live long enough, most likely you will have several of these experiences. However, there is usually one that is pivotal. That which you measure all things against, the before-you and the after-you. It could be a divorce, the hell of separating assets and children, dividing everything you have believed to be true in your life for the last however many years. Tainting the images you have of the early days with your partner making out on park benches and spending all night in bed just talking after you made love. The words that so honestly said forever as you stood before family and friends to publicly declare your love and commit until death do you part. You believe in the forever you were promised on that day. In the images of sipping lemonade on porch swings When you are old and gray, watching the wind gently move the fall leaves on the giant oak tree in your front lawn.

That loss will change a person. Make you question every decision you make moving forward, every butterfly you feel in your stomach when you meet someone for the first time, every expression of love that is given you no matter who it's from. The after from divorce cuts to the bone with an angry knife you never in your wildest dreams thought was possible from the partner you once shared a bathroom sink with, slept naked next to, had babies with. It's a side of humans that is hard to imagine, even though you have seen it again and again from others around you. It still knocks the wind from your lungs.

Or maybe it's the tragic loss of a loved one. A life cut short, causing yours to course-correct in ways you never imagined possible. You believed in the idea of forever. You question every part of life itself, and you throw punches at the sky cursing the God you believed would keep your loved ones safe. Why did this happen? Why are you left here to suffer on the earth He created and asked to continue to believe He is a loving God?

Much like how our country often thinks of events, like the terror attacks on America on September 11, 2001. There is the pre-9/11 world and the world after. Our minds can never go back to how things were before. Our hearts were shattered into tiny little pieces that would take decades to repair. Some never did.

Very often there are negatives as well as positives that come from these experiences, lessons to guide our perspective in the years of the after. We don't often think so at the time. Only hindsight, therapy, personal development, and spirituality can help us see the good that was there for us in those times.

For me, addiction was the sobering experience. My life before July 1, 2002, and the years after. In the last almost two decades since, there have been other meaningful marks in time creating a before and after reality, but none have been quite as necessary or life-changing as this one. In fact, as a person who never expected to live past the age of thirty, I'd say getting sober was the catalyst for creating three other lives, strengthening a marriage, building a career that has touched hundreds of people, allowing the opportunity to serve and experiencing deep sorrow without the numbing effect of drugs and alcohol. This juncture allowed me the opportunity to create a life worth living.

This story is about how I changed my life. Never alone but always one decision, one sacrifice, one minute at a time, learning how to follow directions and change everything. To paint the full picture, I have to give you some details of where I came from. What I was like in the before, what happened to me along the way, and ultimately what led to ending the addiction. But mostly about what my life is like now. What I have done to live sober.

That means maintaining a marriage, parenting, building a business, and preparing for the empty nest all without substances. How taking care of my health, both mentally and physically, was a critical part of this process. And I haven't yet arrived. I believe I am a sober woman under construction. Carefully planning and executing the suggestions of those who have gone before me and those I deeply respect to make sure I maintain mental and spiritual fitness.

Mostly this story is being told as a message not only of the hope that comes from recovery, that is a given, a miracle really, and a blessing for everyone in your life. But also, as the reality of life as a sober woman. The real struggle, joy, and heartache that comes from living life on life's terms with all of its ugliness and discomfort. This isn't an addiction story, although of course you will hear about it, it's a recovery adventure, one that won't be over until I take my last breath. The actuality of recovering in recovery.

RECOVERING IN RECOVERY

CHAPTER 1

HONESTY, OPEN-MINDEDNESS AND WILLINGNESS ARE THE EASIER SOFTER WAY

ADDICT. ALCOHOLIC. THAT WAS ME. MY LIFE IS A million times different today. It's hard to look back on those times now but it's so important that I do. It's truly unbelievable that was me. I literally feel like I have lived two different lives. It's important, not on a regular basis and not for too long, to remember where I came from. My darkest moments today pale in comparison to even my best days when I was in active addiction.

I did not even want to quit when I did. I am so thankful that life and God and circumstances intervened. When you are young, you can withstand the abuse you do to your body way better than you can later in life. But it still takes a toll. I think of the amazing, earth-shattering, positive accomplishments I could have achieved during that time. Addiction takes away your ability to discern right from wrong; you don't have a conscience anymore. Or you just don't care. At the sub-conscious level, memories are stored and that's what causes shame and guilt. I was raised with good morals and taught never to lie, steal, or cheat. During active addiction, I did all of that. It is what alcoholism does. Addiction takes and takes and takes and leaves behind a mess. The selfishness of it all is incredible when you look back from a recovery standpoint.

Addiction and fear walk hand in hand for every addict. Fear is an ugly emotion and if left untreated will eat you alive. I hope I never forget the feelings of defeat, heartache, and loss I felt throughout my time of active addiction. Today, I am committed to finding ways to keep sharing it. Others are coming out of that valley and need to see that climbing the mountain is possible. Some people are still in the valley. They need hope. When we don't show up in this sober life as real people, with big feelings, vulnerable, raw, and exposed, others who are walking the path don't benefit. Shame is a prevalent and difficult emotion for every addict who steps into recovery. Shame prevents people from being transparent, opening up to others, and having deep, meaningful relationships.

I didn't know who I really was. This seems to be true for many addicts. Recovery is a time to change so much beyond abstinence from alcohol. It's time to do healing work from your past trauma or difficult relationships. It's time to discover who you are without substances. So many of us started using mood-altering chemicals from a young age; we are stunted in emotional growth. There was a reliance on drugs and alcohol that prevented the feeling of loss, disappointment, or anger. Substances were a crutch.

Do you do this alone? Of course not. You work hard to stay sober; you change everything. You might choose to work the steps, go to meetings, follow a workbook, connect with other people, hire a coach or go to rehab. Most people who are trying to change will struggle. That in no way means it's wrong, or that they are bad or flawed. We are never done growing or changing; we are all under construction. One blessing of sobriety is the gift of conscience and visceral reactions to circumstances. This awareness is deepened because we are no longer escaping our lives using substances and are now feeling the feelings that come while experiencing the world around us.

Sponsorship is another gift in recovery programs. My first sponsor was an angel. She taught me that AA wasn't the only way to get sober, but it was the only way she knew. I loved that phrase and instilled it in my mind because it's important and honest and true. There are other ways to get sober. There are other ways to heal from trauma, other ways to lose weight, manage money, fix a marriage, raise kids, and train your dog. There are more than a thousand ways to do most things. Yet sometimes, some people believe so strongly in what they are doing, that they forget they are only one person in a whole universe. In fact, there are people that haven't yet been born that will intuitively learn or create new ways to do a ton of the things you do now, but they will be different.

This concept is one of the cornerstones of my recovery life. It is a principle I hold near and dear to my heart and helped me tremendously as I started parenting, matured into adulthood, worked with people in my clinical practice, and showed up online to build a recovery space for women of all walks of life. There are other ways to do your thing. I got sober in AA because that's what was presented to me. And it was the same way for my first sponsor.

Your journey is your own. Whether you got sober using a twelve-step program, your church, or just your own will, you need other tools in your life. The toolbox that worked in early sobriety may feel a bit snug like jeans that are a size too small. Maybe you have cleaned out parts of your life, reduced toxic people, gotten rid of the abusive partner, gone back to school, or had a baby. You have more work to do. Be willing to take action. It takes a while. I have had internal tantrums fighting against the changes that were necessary because I didn't want to make adjustments. Resistance has to be smashed, but often it takes someone else to help us.

It is shocking to see the negative self-talk most women are struggling with on a regular basis. I certainly have experienced negative thinking patterns, and even today continue to work at dismantling any that come in. If you want to learn 5 *Ways To Change Your Negative Thinking*, go to www.shelbyjohncoaching.com/negativethinking.

I assumed that no one was as sick as me. Most of the women I encounter in the sober community have struggled with limiting beliefs that hold them back from having the confidence they want and need to go after their desires or even just speak up for what they need. So many of us aren't taught about our personal needs, nor are we given permission to have them. We just carry on with the stories we are told about ourselves and later replay them over and over like a broken record. The neural pathways in our brains store these thought patterns based on the trauma we experience throughout life. Without intervention and retraining, they stay on repeat for our whole lives. Those negative thought patterns affect your relationships, your professional life, and your ability to create healthy boundaries.

I have not had a drink in almost twenty years. I am still in recovery and would love to bring every addict with me, up out of the pit and into the mountain climb of recovery. I know today that honesty, open-mindedness, and willingness are the easier softer way to living well beyond recovery. Lessons and truths and growth have been gifts to me along the way. They are here to share with you.

CHAPTER 2

ADDICTION ISN'T A CHOICE, BUT RECOVERY IS.

JULY 1, 2002, WAS THE FIRST DAY OF MY SECOND life. The beginning of the after.

I had no idea it was coming. I wasn't the kind of drunk who knew it was the end, who said it wasn't working anymore or wanted help. Although I would imagine if you had asked anyone close to me, they would have said hands down, yes, I had a problem with alcohol.

What I know today is usually we are the last to know. There are incidents, accidents, institutional involvements, loss of relationships, and health problems long before we reach the end of our drinking. That was certainly my story. I struggled with difficult emotions for years before reaching this point. I embarrassed my husband at professional functions, placed myself in dangerous situations more times than I would care to admit, and I was depressed and anxious. I didn't know I was depressed and anxious at the time, but I did know something was different about me inside.

It wasn't the kind of difference that was clearly noticeable to others. On the outside, I followed the general layout of "normal" American life checking off the boxes. There were some quirky things, but nothing abnormal. I wasn't labeled the weird kid in high school or a freak. In fact, my mom told me often she heard from other moms that I was popular. Their daughters looked up to me, I was with the "in" crowd. Hearing this as an adult took me aback as I didn't think of myself in that way at all. I knew the girls in my friend group were very beautiful, athletic, and smart but in no way did I believe I was popular. Nor would I have attached any of those adjectives to a description of myself.

My last drunk was the most eventful of all. I was a high-functioning drinker with the usual embarrassing moments. Blackouts, regrets, depression. I graduated college, got a master's degree, was married, owned a home, worked full time and had friends. I was living out what I was taught was the order life should go in. I drank to excess almost daily, but I never had serious consequences. No DUI's, although I drove drunk a lot, and no legal problems. But this last drunk was a real doozy.

In late June of that year, I attended a conference in Washington, D.C. with hundreds of social workers, other helping professionals, and foster care youth learning the life skills necessary for being released from the system at the age of 21. I can't even remember what the conference was about, what workshops I attended, or who I was with.

I couldn't say the name of the hotel where I stayed or really any details about those few days. I wasn't drunk the whole time, but I was very much in the grips of raging addiction and depression that left me more of a shell of a person than whole. Alcoholism stole large sections of my memory that I have not regained even to this day.

One night during the conference, I went out to dinner. I don't know what restaurant it was or if I was with anyone, but I was drinking. Of course, I was drinking. I was able to expense the meal for work, so I had more cash to spend on alcohol.

I was twenty-six years old, had a master's degree in social work, and had been working for the Department of Social Services in Maryland for over four years. I worked in the foster care division with youth who were preparing to age out. The job was fulfilling and fun because I was young. When I started, I was close in age to the teens I served.

I regularly planned events like graduation parties, etiquette retreats, and life skills workshops to teach young people how to manage life in adulthood. I loved it. I loved planning for them and connecting with them. I was in awe of the trauma they had endured and the loyalty many of them still had for their birth families.

These children were warriors. They were the real deal of what happens when people who shouldn't have children continue to do so, then commit horrific atrocities against their kids, and lose those children to the state. The kids who could get through their teen years without much trouble, took advantage of the free college tuition they were given by the government, or found gainful employment, gave us as their caseworkers hope and kept us going. Kept me going. Sadly, many didn't enjoy such success. Despite planning, training, and the love we poured into them, the cycle continued. It was a thankless job, filled with just as much heartbreak as joy. It was soul-sucking at times.

Once or twice a year, I took the teens to conferences all around the country that were designed for them and the adults who worked on their behalf. It afforded me the opportunity to travel around the county and share those experiences with foster care youth who often hadn't even traveled outside the county they lived in. I can remember one such trip when I took an older teen with me. We went to New Mexico for a youth conference. She and I had a good relationship, and I was newer in the job. We were close in age. At dinner one night during our trip, I can remember ordering a beer. I knew I probably shouldn't drink because that was inappropriate when traveling for work with a ward of the state. But I did it. I even asked her if she wanted one! Definitely not appropriate. I remember buying some bottled beer after dinner to take back to the hotel with us.

Thankfully, despite my offerings, this smart girl respectfully declined. The night was uneventful from there, but it left a stain of regret on my heart for years after I got sober. I couldn't believe my own lapses in common sense. The lack of judgement was preposterous, and yet it happened repeatedly.

That night at the conference in D.C. wasn't any different. The details of that evening are foggy at best, I was a regular black-out drinker, so this wasn't unusual. I had lost many a night to the oblivion of my drunken stupor. I sometimes had to tiptoe through my house looking for evidence of what went on and apologize more often than I can count for the shenanigans I had engaged in while under the influence, most of which I never remembered.

What I do remember is walking back to the hotel and waking up in my room. I have flashes of the hallway but no other real memory of anything or anyone that I encountered. The next day I woke up, quite hungover, took a shower, put on a long comfy wine-colored sundress, and headed downstairs for the conference. Sometime during the day, my name was called on the loudspeaker to report to the office in the lobby. I remember we were in a keynote speaker session. It was a large conference room with several round tables of professional colleagues. It felt surreal, almost dreamlike. At some point, two police officers were asking me questions and then parading me out of the hotel. They put me into a police car and took me to a Washington, D.C. police station for questioning. I had no idea why.

At the police station, I was put into a room with two police officers. One was in plain clothes so likely a detective. They asked me question after question about the events of the prior evening. I do not even remember this interrogation, except for watching that taped session in a fancy D.C. lawyer's office over a month later. Not from any real memory.

The next thing I knew I was in a jail cell with several other women. I was a 26-year-old white woman in a wine-colored sundress and sandals in a jail cell in Washington, D.C. To say I stood out would have been an understatement. I was curled up in a ball, sobbing. When I think back on this time today, I often wonder what those other women were thinking about this blonde-haired, blue-eyed, white girl wearing a sundress, bawling in a jail cell. It was likely laughable. At some point that night, they moved me to a different police station. I have no idea why or where, but it was more of the same. I was told that I would be having a court hearing in the morning in front of a judge, and I was appointed a public defender. I barely remember speaking with this man, and at that point, I hadn't made any contact with my husband or family.

A phone call was also made to my employer. When I arrived at the courthouse, women I worked with at social services were standing in the courtroom. I remember wondering during my early recovery, why would they have come all the way down there? Why did they care so much about me? Yet there they were, standing on my behalf as witnesses to my character and sound mind. I can't even imagine the shock they must have felt receiving a phone call like this. Not exactly a great

when you are in the midst of active addiction. That is in fact the problem, right? I wasn't aware that past events and childhood trauma affect the brain to create dysfunctional neural pathways. When negative beliefs formulated from those events were not processed properly, they got threaded throughout the rest of my life. They affected my relationships, professional development, physical health, and ability to experience true joy.

The research that has been done over the past two decades clearly reveals the effect of trauma on the brain. Scientists have used scans to disclose where the damage lies and the impact to our dopamine receptors, serotonin levels and emotional centers. In addition, we know that Adverse Childhood Experiences (ACEs), traumatic events that occur in childhood from ages 0 to 17, are linked to chronic health problems, mental health, and substance abuse in adulthood. ACEs can negatively impact a child's education, future job opportunities, and earning potential, yet we know they can be prevented.

A friend of a friend contacted an attorney in the D.C. area to advise us and decide the best course of action. The attorney was a kind man, competent, and a bit fancy. Ryan and I drove to his office to discuss with him all that had happened and make a plan for what to do. I remember being nervous, embarrassed, and scared. What was going to happen to me? Would I lose my job? Was I going to rehab? I had so many questions. Self-centered questions about my own life, the consequences, and potential loss. I couldn't turn my attention to those around me who were incredibly impacted by these actions. This is the difference between being in addiction and working on recovery.

The interrogation tape we watched during that meeting is burned into my mind. Similar to what you see on television but a whole lot less exciting when it's you sitting in the room. The police officers questioned me, and the interrogation was recorded. The lawyer had obtained the tape from the police department, and we watched it in his upscale office together. I had no idea at the time, but this would become one of the pivotal moments in my recovery. Something I would refer back to again and again. The gist of what happened during that interview is the police consistently asked me about my drinking. Where had I been? How much had I drunk? What had happened? For forty-five minutes I explained to them over and over and over again how I hadn't been drunk that night. I knew what I was like when I was drunk. That hadn't been it. Watching the tapes was gut-wrenching. As I sat there in an uppity law office in D.C. with my husband watching me on screen, the reality that my drinking was a serious problem had never been clearer. I hope I never forget it.

With efforts from both Ryan and my parents, a bed was found for me in an amazing treatment program in our area. I was soon checked into rehab. I was filled with overwhelming fear and anxiety. I knew what alcoholism was, I was educated after all. And despite slogans like "one day at a time," I knew that this really meant that I couldn't drink forever. That was paralyzing and sent my mind into an immediate panic, watching my future life like a movie flash before me with all the events, experiences, relationships, and feelings that would be without alcohol. I was naïve to the realities of the enormity of that concept, and I had nothing to compare it to. No parent, distant cousin, friend or coworker I knew that was an alcoholic or addict had gotten sober. All I knew was most people in my life drank heavily, that alcohol was completely normalized and necessary to function in adulthood and no one in the world would ever choose to be sober. That was definitely not something I was interested in at the time. I was compliant with going to treatment because it didn't seem like I had a whole lot of other options. My family was saying this was necessary. My relationships were surface at best because of my inability to identify my own feelings, let alone be vulnerable enough to share them with those close to me. My insurance company however didn't agree. We had to borrow a large sum of money for inpatient treatment from my parents.

The lack of financial resources for treatment for those who don't have health insurance or funds to pay for it was astounding to me. Phrases like "you aren't sick enough to need rehab," or "this is your first try so we aren't going to pay" lit me up with anger at the system. How sick did they want me to be? How dead did they need me to be in order to deem my treatment necessary? We did everything it took. My addiction had not been a choice for years because for those who struggle with substance abuse there comes a time when we lose that choice to drink or use. My body and mind became physically addicted to the substance and I saw no way out of that. Up until that point short of a few passing comments to go to AA, I hadn't really tried.

For years I made the decision to continue the cycle of addiction without acknowledging it. Until I was taught that I had a problem with alcohol that centered in my mind and my body, that it wasn't my fault and I couldn't control it, my life would get worse, never better if I continued. I learned that making the decision to put any substances in my body the very first time was the last time I had any choice regarding addiction. None of us know whether or not we will become addicted to substances. We can't know. There isn't a blood test to show if in fact you choose to take a drink in someone's basement when you are fifteen years old, with kids you have known your whole life, in order to feel like you fit in, that eventually you will become an addict. The only way to know is to make a decision to take the first drink. Beyond that, addiction is not a choice. But recovery is. I made that choice with intention, stepped into recovery and never looked back.

CHAPTER 3

WHAT HAPPENED TO YOU ISN'T YOUR FAULT, BUT HEALING IS YOUR RESPONSIBILITY.

WHEN I WAS FIVE YEARS OLD, MY BIOLOGICAL father left my mother. He was having an affair with one of my mother's friends. My mom was twenty-six years old. She didn't have a job and a limited college education. My sister was two years old, and I was five. She was completely blindsided by this betrayal. I can only imagine the feelings of horror she must have endured. The fear of what the future would bring. How would she take care of two little ones on her own?

When I became a mother myself, my admiration and complete awe of my mom, and what she worked through during that time, grew stronger. I couldn't imagine getting through those events the way she did. Her parents lived outside of Philadelphia. They were supportive of her, but in more of the "pull yourself up by your bootstraps and figure it out" kind of way. That's exactly what she did.

My mom stayed in the house we had all lived in with our dad. she found a job and a roommate, another newly single woman with a daughter my age. My father didn't want anything from my mom including his daughters. He just wanted out so he could be with the other woman. He told my mother she could have the house and us girls, and he paid her a small amount of child support each month plus more for our education. The only recollection I have from that time is my father kneeling down in front of me and saying he was leaving to go to his mother's house to cut wood. He never came back.

We visited with him on the weekends but every time we went to his house, he would be working. He left us with the other woman. I don't have any fond memories of this woman during that time. In fact, I can only recall criticism about us. He wasn't engaged in our lives; he wasn't interested. My sister Leslie and I would call him at times, but he wouldn't take our calls. We visited our father soon after he left our family, but then called our mother and the man who would become our stepfather to come pick us up. We wanted to go home. I don't remember ever going back.

He sent birthday cards, paid tuition, and gave money for medical bills and for some summer camps. He married the other woman. They had two sons who we never met. He lived in our county about 25 minutes away. I don't remember my mom ever speaking badly about him. To me, this is one of her most admirable character traits. From where I sit today as a wife and mother of three children, I know from the depths of my gut how hard that was. In fact, it would have been within her rights to have full-out rages against this man who publicly humiliated her and kicked her to the curb like last week's garbage. The heartache and pain of betrayal leave a trauma stain for sure, how can it not? The trust issues that come with unfaithfulness are real and lasting. I respect the way she handled it and often share this with my clients today who are going through similar situations and tempted (or already have) to use their children as sounding boards for their own pain. Calling names, giving their parent certain trendy labels, and posting about them on social media. All of this is so damaging and considered adverse childhood events which we know from years of research are contributing factors to addiction. All she ever said was, "Someday you might want to get to know him."

At one point, my stepdad (although we have never ever used that term in our family) wanted to adopt us. He and my mom had a child together now, our brother Johnny. My stepdad wanted us to be a family. He and my mom reached out to my biological father about it. My father would not agree to that. It was confusing then. In hindsight, he likely had his own guilt and sadness that had been left unhealed. Ultimately, we benefited financially, emotionally, and spiritually from him saying no. My parents were innovative. They created their own "adoption" for us. They had a friend who knew calligraphy. They asked her to make beautiful adoption certificates for us, and we had a special dinner with our family. We hung those certificates in our rooms where they stayed until we left home. It is true the family is whatever you make it. I was blessed to have one.

As a social worker I learned that children do seek their parents. There is a sort of hole in the soul that forms when a parent is absent or unknown. During my time, working at Social Services I saw more of this in both our foster care youth and kids who had been adopted. Despite where they came from, they wanted to know their parents. In modern times we see evidence of this with the evolution of programs like 23 And Me or Ancestry.com. Some are naturally curious about their roots, want to know about their ancestors and track the history of their family line. But many are using it to search for parents or siblings they never knew. This void, this lack of knowledge is a trauma that needs to be healed. For many women, lack of connection with their parents leaves them feeling abandoned (even if they were raised in supportive and loving homes). Unfortunately, there is a snowball effect from there to beliefs about themselves, their value and worth but most significantly belonging. And young people who struggle with feeling like they were abandoned and don't belong tend to fall prey to the use of substances to take away the discomfort, stop their own negative thinking patterns and simply fit in. They want to be wanted. This is the perfect breeding ground for addiction.

I longed to know my birth father. I felt a void in my soul, a deep inner longing to know where they came from and understand their DNA. Even though he had done a terrible thing and as a younger person, I couldn't completely wrap my head around all of it because of lack of experience the desire was there. This was true for me, despite the perfectly loving and supportive family I had. I experienced deep hurt and feelings of abandonment. Why would my father just leave his two children behind? Didn't he wonder what we were doing? Did he care what we now looked like? Did it matter to him who we were? These questions plagued me for years and I believed I wasn't worthy of love. I believed I did something wrong, that it was my fault. These irrational thoughts were stored in my brain and nurtured for years carving deep neuropathways that would affect my relationships, my confidence and ability to pursue my own desires. Oh and of course a beautiful recipe for substance abuse.

Despite the obvious dysfunction, he came from a wealthy family. My sister and I, along with his other two children from his second marriage, were the only grandchildren. My paternal grandfather, who died an alcoholic death at a young age, was quite successful and had saved a significant amount of money in a trust fund. That fund was designed for the education of the grandchildren. I believe my father took this into consideration when he said no to the adoption.

My siblings and I grew up like many suburban families in the 1980s. We ran the streets of our neighborhood until the streetlights came on, rented VHS tapes every weekend, and ate frozen pizza. We went roller skating every Friday night at Skateland. We walked to the school every day, to the local convenience store and pizza parlor and skated in the neighborhood, holding the back of the banana seat on our friends' bikes while our long unmanaged hair flowed in the wind. We had a lot of unsupervised fun; we were happy. My parents moved us to a neighboring community when I was in the 7th grade. We switched to the local public school. I had a fairly typical middle school experience, with awkward stages of big bangs and braces. I was an average student who really cared more about playing club soccer than grades. I wore my Guess Jeans, Benetton sweaters and Swatch watches with pride.

I was bullied in middle school. This was long before bullying was emphasized the way it is now. The girl was stealing my lunch, taking my lunch money, and pushing me around in the bathroom. The story was that I "fell" into the trash can. My parents found out and marched up to school to meet with the principal. He informed them the girl was a sixteen-year-old eighth grader. Naturally, they were furious that a girl this much older was in middle school with students so much younger. Apparently, Dad asked what a sixteen-year-old was doing in a middle school? As a parent now, I can completely understand.

There were other shenanigans that went on but mostly the innocent type. I was a good kid, under the radar, no real concern. I also had a strong-willed sister who was in elementary school and challenged her new teachers, plus a three-year-old brother. My parents were busy. I like to believe I made it easy for them. Throughout the years we would hear tales about our biological father. We lived in the same community so there was some crossover with his circle of friends and with some of his extended family who also lived in that county. Sometimes we would wonder what our brothers were like. It felt strange to know we had two other siblings, yet we hadn't even met them. I didn't even know what they looked like. We had no contact with them, except for the occasional awkward sighting in town or at a restaurant.

How could a dad just walk away? In time, I learned that what he did truly was a gift. The abandonment left a trauma stain on our brains. The negative beliefs that developed in us then morphed into things like addiction, depression and anxiety and cultivated a need for therapy. But what he gave us was the opportunity to live and be raised in a loving two-parent family without the perils that children of divorced parents typically face. We did not deal with going back and forth between homes, sharing holidays, fighting over custody, child support issues, etc. My kids today share about their friends keeping clothes in the trunks of their car because they are always going back and forth. One of them even thanked me once for not doing that to them. I view his choice to stay out of our lives as a perfectly planned blessing from God. It took me a long time to learn that none of this was my fault. It wasn't my sister's fault, nor was it my mom's fault. The realization that it was not even my biological dad's fault took even longer. Even though it was not my fault, I did have some baggage that was my responsibility. Instead of dealing with that baggage at the time, I carried it and drank over it for far too long.

CHAPTER 4

IN RECOVERY, NOTHING CHANGES IF YOU DON'T CHANGE.

A T THE START OF HIGH SCHOOL, I CONTINUED to play sports but was a little awkward. I was in the popular group, however I would never have thought that at the time. I wasn't really "in" the popular group, more like I was around them. I remember starting to feel a bit out of place, uncomfortable in my own skin. The obvious differences between the girls who cared about hair and make-up versus my baggy clothes and an almost tomboyish style became clear.

My parents were aware of what we did socially. They had expectations, and they set rules. My mom called the other parents when I wanted to spend the night or go to parties with friends. We weren't allowed to go out on school nights and or watch too much television. The shows we did watch once a week were wholesome, family-based sitcoms. I was an average student. Grades were a bit of a focus growing up. My parents wanted us to do well. They encouraged hard work in school, expected college enrollment, and rewarded us for good progress. I remember many report card reward dinners at one of the fancier establishments in the area.

The awkwardness I felt seemed greater than that of my friends. I started to struggle with self-esteem. I lacked the confidence my peers seemed to exhibit in athletics and socially. I started to dislike myself deeply.

The summer before my junior year, I started dating the man who would become my husband. We were in the same group of friends, but he was different. Much smarter, more cautious, and much more confident than I was. And he was very handsome. The prior school year he had his eye on the girl who was sitting next to him in chemistry class. I was on the other side. The story goes that he pursued this girl and was rejected so he turned the other way. Toward the end of the year, he helped me with my homework. When school let out for summer, we connected at a party. We soon started dating and the rest is history. My parents loved Ryan because he was a good boy. He was smart, ambitious, had a good reputation, and had a job. He checked all the boxes that a parent would want in a partner for their daughter. They accepted him into our family right away, and that Christmas he joined us for our family celebration.

Ryan and I had many differences, but I think that's what made us such a good match. One major contrast was that he wanted to go to a small college where he would have more personal attention from his professors and be recognized for his success. I wanted the exact opposite of that—I wanted to be invisible. My self-esteem was fairly non-existent at this point, and I had no desire for any professor to know me. That would have meant I would be accountable to them, they might check up on me and see how I was doing, why I wasn't in class or why I had failed an exam. No thank you. A large school as far away as my parents would let me go, where no one knew my name was the only option.

Our senior year as we were working through the college process, my mom, stepdad, and father discussed tuition and funding that was available for college through my grandfather's trust. My parents were working with my father until one day, there was a heated discussion between my biological father and my dad. I don't know what happened, but he turned the process over to my mom and I from that point. We planned to meet with my biological father at his office. It had been ten years since I had seen him. My stomach was in knots. This initial meeting led to him providing the funding for my college expenses and us getting back in touch.

That was the year I started to experiment with alcohol. My use was fairly minimal at first. My parents always waited up for me. They made it clear if they caught me drinking, using drugs, or if I came home one minute past my curfew, I would be punished. I was always the designated driver, and I would cart Ryan and his drunk friends around while they did things like moon people out the rear window. Teenage boys were fun.

Although they had always been there at some level, the negative beliefs and self-hate were building by late high school. My body image issues increased during this time as well. I never felt like I fit in. I never felt like I was enough. I was an athletic girl with soccer legs who couldn't take a compliment from anyone. This is when the lies really began. Saying I was fine when I knew I wasn't. Reversing anything positive anyone said to me and internalizing the belief that I was worthless. I was a girl that lived in constant chaos. I look back now and can see a lot of discontentment, discomfort, and spiraling that started at a young age. Thankfully, I was raised in a loving family who provided a lot of opportunities. The dysfunctional parts of me remained under the radar and were not able to grow into a full-blown mental health problem until much later. Now I can see what was going on was anxiety; we just didn't call it that back then.

By the end of my senior year in high school, my alcohol use increased. It seemed fun at the time. The tendencies and insecurities were already there, and my brain was just waiting for something to come in and give it the relief it so desperately was seeking at seventeen years old. Many teenagers experiment with substances and don't end up as addicts. The problem with substance abuse is you don't know if you are an addict until you put the substance in your body. That first drink is a choice, what happens after may not be. You don't know if you will have the addictive response to alcohol unless you open that door and walk through. Once you do, you can't go back.

My trip to the beach for senior week would now be considered a serious red flag. It's not a trip I remember fondly. There was a large amount of alcohol consumption, and I showed no care or concern for my own personal safety. We rented a small house, but I never even spent the night there. We went to parties, fried our skin on the beach, and nursed hangovers while we drank more. I don't remember much of the behavior of my friends during that week. Mine was out of control. One night on that beach trip there was drama going on, likely related to me and my then ex-boyfriend Ryan. He was still upset that I had broken up with him right before graduation and knew I was acting in a way that was flirtatious and frankly dangerous. Since we were in the same friend group, he was around during that trip, he was very aware of my state of mind and behavior. I found myself walking on the boardwalk alone in the middle of the night, bawling and praying to die. Obviously, it's not safe for a young girl to be walking around alone in a beach town and certainly not in emotional distress. But that's where my head was. I was slipping fast into the depths of depression, and alcohol was accelerating that process. There were other shenanigans, including me running in front of a moving bus to try and catch it, but by the grace of God somehow, I got home alive.

Soon after that trip, I left for college. I chose a large university in North Carolina so I could be invisible on campus and a few hours from home. I was looking for an escape by then, not only from my hometown but from myself. A geographical change. I wanted to go where no one knew my name. I lived in a huge dorm on the fifteenth floor with no air conditioning. It's hot in North Carolina. We ran the window fans nonstop and struggled to sleep at night because we were sweating in our beds. The long autumns and mild winters made being there worth it. I met some friends, drank a lot, was introduced to marijuana, and learned how to drive a stick shift. That only happened because I was the most sober person one night leaving a bar. I remember calling home and being sad, missing my family. My mom gave me her best pull-yourself-up-and-get-it-done type of advice. Emotionally, I wasn't well. I attended classes, got mediocre grades, went to all the school's basketball games, and drank through it all. I wasn't any different from anyone else around me at the time, at least not on the outside. They were all partying the same way.

I didn't have a car at the time, but Ryan did. He would come down to visit often. We traveled the area around my campus. I got to see The Biltmore, Gatlinburg, Tennessee, and we went east to see the beaches and the colleges there. I would fly home to visit Ryan at his college and became close with his friends there. There were many memorable times. He had a group of guy friends that were pretty tight. We would all drink and party together, but my drinking was always a little different. I was the girl that would get drunk and then show my boobs to all those guys or throw up so I could keep drinking.

On the inside I was slowly dying. My spirit was being crushed by the weight of my own discomfort and substance abuse. I didn't care about myself. I was restricting my calories because I hated my body. I was reckless, ended up in places I had no business being, struggled to make connections with others. I was stuck in my own sickness.

Back in those days, we didn't have cell phones. We were still writing letters. Email was just emerging, but we had to go to a computer lab across campus to check it. We had landline phones attached to walls with cords, paid long distance fees and we used calling cards. I would get drunk at a party off campus, then use the land line phone to call Ryan or a friend and talk to them for hours. I was racking up long distance phone bills all over town. Eventually I was called out on it when friends' phone bills started getting higher and higher.

Miraculously, I did well in school. I was told before leaving for college some of the best advice I think anyone could give—go to every class no matter what. That way at least you are there to learn and absorb the material, even if you don't study much. I did work hard; we pulled many all-nighters with caffeine pills and chili dogs. My memories aren't clear about my time in North Carolina, just a few spotty images and a recollection of the deep dread, self-hate, and lack of esteem that was always present. I think I had some friends, but nothing substantial. I remember struggling to get along with my suitemates.

My second year there, my mental health continued to go downhill. There was conflict among my friends. I was deeply depressed, and I started hoarding sleeping pills in my underwear drawer. I wasn't new to thoughts of suicide. I had suicidal ideations in high school for brief periods, but they came and went. Now I had a plan. Ryan and I broke up for a time and dated other people. I chose the most glamorous losers I could find. I dated a guy who lived in a fraternity house. He was well into his twenties and should have been long gone from college. There were no other real relationships, only drunken party blackout flings. I didn't know how to be in a relationship. I didn't feel worthy of love from others. I didn't know how to connect with other humans, and I knew they wouldn't like me for who I really was, so I felt why bother?

Sometime that year, I became so depressed I took all the sleeping pills I had hidden. I just wanted to escape. Even though most days I wanted to die, I wasn't sure if I truly desired to be gone forever. I needed to get out of the discomfort that was my life; I needed a break, wanted to check out, wanted to sleep. I remember at some point waking up, stumbling into a tiny bathroom stall and barfing my guts out. I had no idea where I was. I saw black. I made it to my bed and slept for an entire day and night. When I woke up the first thought I had was "Wow, what a loser, I even failed at killing myself." I never told anyone about it. Shortly after that incident, an acquaintance asked if I wanted to join the crew team. I had zero idea what that even was. The crew team practiced at 5 am daily, and it sounded like insanity to me. But extremes, athletics, opportunities to beat myself up were my specialty. I said yes. In the spring semester of my sophomore year at North Carolina State University, I was on the crew team, and it saved my life. I had no idea at the time, but this was actually the hand of God Himself throwing me a life vest.

Somewhere in that time I also made the decision to leave that school and finish college closer to home, closer to Ryan. I transferred to Towson State University near my hometown and lived in an apartment with a high school friend. Towson even had a crew team. I was thrilled because I was now obsessed with the sport and wanted to continue. This became my life, my structure, and my focus outside of school. Ryan was academically focused, so we didn't spend much time together during the week. Crew became my focus. When I got to Towson, my issues with perfectionism and body image took on a life of their own. The food restrictions increased drastically. There were times when my roommate and I literally lived on carrots, pretzels, and diet soda. I remember having a constant focus on my weight and food and using the circumference of my wrist to measure progress. I was obsessed with working out. The crew team often worked out twice a day, and we traveled together on the weekends to regattas. Thank God for those people; they became like family. I wasn't eating much, was getting up at 4:00 am to work out, going to school, and trying to maintain a relationship. I decided to become the president of the crew team to help take it to another level. There were times I would go off the wagon with food. I would tell myself, "You are a failure at anorexia, you can't get thin enough. You wouldn't even qualify for help at this point because you aren't thin enough." I was drinking and smoking and trying to maintain it all.

I also discovered laxatives as a weight-loss tool. Not sure why this is a tool that people use, because it's incredibly gross. I felt that I was failing at food restriction, so I sought another resource. I guess because of embarrassment and because I didn't have much money, I stole laxatives from grocery stores. I would stand in the aisle and take the foil packs out of the boxes and put them in my pockets, leaving the box on the shelf. I did that many times. I took more than the recommended dosage to clean out my system as often as necessary, especially when I gave in to the nagging temptation of food.

While I had found a meaningful relationship with Ryan and deeply loved him, I continued in the patterns of substance abuse and escape. Even though we were moving forward toward marriage, I sustained the trauma and pain of my childhood—my baggage. The insanity of all things—addiction was my life. I lied to myself and others because it was impossible for me to get honest. I couldn't see the harm I was doing to myself, in fact, in my view, I was doing all the right things. And I certainly had no idea how my actions affected those who loved me. I was a living, breathing example of the truth that if nothing changes, then nothing changes.

CHAPTER 5

THERE IS MUCH LOVE TO GIVE AND RECEIVE IN THIS WORLD, AND IT'S WORTH IT.

I N MAY OF MY JUNIOR YEAR, I WENT TO THE FAMOUS Triple Crown horse race, The Preakness, at the Pimlico racetrack in Baltimore. It was common for college students to attend this event but not in fancy dresses and beautiful hats like you see on television. We were on the infield. In fact, we took school busses from designated locations that were loaded with coolers and trash cans full of beer to the racetrack that left at 8:00 a.m. It was May, so the weather was sunny and hot. Thousands of college students started drinking for breakfast, filling an area bigger than an NFL football field. What could go wrong? Guys tossed girls up in the air in blankets, porta-pots got tipped over with people in them, and most of us never saw a horse all day. It was what we called fun.

That year after the Preakness, I remember walking home with a friend who lived in apartments close to the track. It was challenging to get transportation from the racetrack back home, so we decided to walk. In my drunken state, I became flooded with emotion over who knows what and quickly spiraled into the depths of a depressive episode. As we walked across an overpass above the highway, I imagined jumping off that bridge. I shared that with my friend. She was alarmed but supportive and listened to me cry. She listened to me recount the perils of my privileged, addicted life. It was scary because I was completely serious. How scary that must have been for her. A friend who likely knew me fairly well, but only the parts I allowed to show through. The dark side remained hidden except in moments like these made vulnerable only by the overuse of alcohol. The hope of recovery tells us things never have to be that way again. The double life can be merged like the two pieces of bread in a perfectly made peanut butter and jelly sandwich. They were made for each other.

That night I laid on the floor of her apartment and wept until I fell asleep or passed out. People cared about me, loved me and my life looked full from the outside. There were parts of me that so desperately wanted the loving acceptance of others, that deeply desired the kind of connections that form and allow for total raw honesty. But there was no way for me to live in that skin. I was almost finished with college, I had a smart, handsome, and kind fiancé, but I was dead on the inside. Unable to receive all that love in a way that would make me want to live. Empty.

In October of our senior year in college, Ryan proposed to me with the blessing of my parents, a heart full of love, and a bag of apples. We were twenty-one years old, babies really. We were in love as much as we knew how to be at the time, and the next logical step was marriage. We knew we wanted to move in together after graduation, and it would be easier to get that past his parents if we were engaged.

On our first date, June 21, 1991, he took me to the movies to see *Backdraft*. I didn't even have a driver's license. When I got home that night, I remember saying to my mom, "I'm going to marry him." I knew it would happen. We were born to be together despite my raging addiction, incredible dysfunction, and emotional unavailability. He was my first love, and I know God perfectly planned our union to save my life and provide an amazing future family. We had college to finish, and now we were adding the stress of wedding planning. Thankfully, my mom, who was younger than I am now, was great at planning parties and just as excited as we were. I was still on the crew team, finishing my senior year, and making exceptionally poor life decisions. My conscience was wiped out at this point, and I was living a double life. I have no idea how I graduated. I have no recollection of any classes I took, where they were located on campus, or really anything from that time. Except the pain. The emotional pain was excruciating.

Ryan and I began making plans for moving in together and finding jobs. He planned to study for the CPA exam. I planned to work until he could take the exam. A few months before we were scheduled to get married, we almost ended our engagement for good. My drinking progressed even further. I was living a delusion and couldn't keep track of my own lies. I was disconnected emotionally, making terrible choices with my time and my body. I couldn't communicate properly. Therefore, the conversations about my substance abuse and mental health never happened with Ryan. This man was my partner since I was sixteen years old. We spent most of our time together, enjoyed holidays, shared a bed, we were engaged to be married. He had loved me through it all, supported me, and shared his feelings and dreams with me as we made plans for our future. But I couldn't do the same for him. I wasn't brave enough to fully open up about everything that was going on in my head. Or maybe I just didn't get it at all. Something had to give. He called all his friends (they were my friends as well by this time) to come and help him move his belongings out of our apartment. I couldn't blame him really. Part of me thought, "Yeah, you should run, Ryan. Run far away from me." I also knew I couldn't live without him; I wouldn't live without him. Somewhere deep in his soul, I knew he felt the same way. That night there was crying and fighting but thankfully both finally stopped. We worked it out, and his poor friends had to move his belongings back in.

As a psychology major, I needed more school to

get a job in my field. I worked for temp agencies and any other jobs I could find to make money while Ryan prepared for his CPA exam. I needed to pay our rent and buy food while we waited for Ryan to take his exam and start working. I took a job at a failing day care center. The woman who hired me needed someone with a college degree to be the director per state regulations. The office was filled with unpaid bills, trash, and piles of paperwork. I was delusional and thought I could fix that mess. I did clean it up a lot. We renovated and painted and got paperwork filed. I was only there a short time, but I consider it another representation of my settling for less. I needed to know I could do more.

In April 1998, I got a job at the Department of Social Services in my county. I worked in the foster care division. It was a contractual job, meaning no benefits and a meager $20,000 a year salary. There was opportunity, though, to become a full-time employee. Since there weren't many other options, it became my plan. I was twenty-two years old. I loved working with the young people there. I had much to learn, was completely naive to the realities of life for many and had no experience with a government agency. I did have a huge heart and belief that I could change the world. I could show them the way. I'm thankful for that job. I learned volumes and met some great people. and one of my favorite aspects of that job was that I got to travel.

Ryan and I were married June 6, 1998. We had a beautiful wedding with several events and our closest friends and family. The wedding was at 10:45 a.m., so there were mimosas in the morning while we got ready. The weather was gorgeous and everyone looked beautiful. We were 23 years old. The photos are so fun to look through. Our college friends were there, my grandparents were still alive, my little brother was thirteen years old. It was a huge party. I was drinking heavily, like every other day. I was whisked around the whole time and fed drinks, while I visited with each guest. I'm sure I didn't eat a single bite of the incredible food we had catered. At one point, I tripped and fell on one of the door jams. I busted my knee open and got blood on my dress. I always say drinking had nothing to do with it, that it was the raised door jam. I bounced back up, got a Band-Aid and continued partying. We continued the party at my parent's house when the reception ended that afternoon. I passed out in one of the bedrooms upstairs for a while until a bridesmaid woke me up to come back and join the fun. One of the groomsmen played air guitar while lying on the dog and another fell into the pool with all his clothes on.

We lived in a one-bedroom apartment. Ryan studied, I worked, and we lived on very little cash per month. I eventually got the full-time job at social services, and Ryan started working at a public accounting firm. We were a working American couple. Not long after, we found a little starter home in the county where we had grown up. We broke the lease on our apartment to move into that house. It was an exciting time. We seemed happy. We customized the house with paint and hand-me-down furniture, and we got two cats from the Humane Society. I quickly realized after working at social services that it was necessary for me to have a master's degree. Without it, I would not be able to advance professionally. I applied and was admitted to the University of Maryland School of Social Work, and I spent three years completing that degree. The government offered a tuition reimbursement plan for employees for a portion of the tuition. They also provided internships which helped significantly with our finances. The perfectionism that I had begun in college ramped up to a whole new level. I was obsessed with my grades and still struggled with body image issues. I worked out excessively, took laxatives, restricted food and purged after meals.

We now owned two cars, a house, and two cats. We had a recliner, and I remember sitting in that chair with my huge plastic cup full of vodka mixed with whatever we had on hand. It could have been diet soda, orange juice, or iced tea. I'd cry the blues to Sarah McLachlan's *Surfacing* album with the song *Angel* on repeat. Drinking and depression took over my life. We attended one of our friend's parties in the summer of 2001 with some of Ryan's college friends. I was an emotional drunk and got into an argument with Ryan. When we got home, I took a massive amount of painkillers and sleeping pills. Ryan found me, called an ambulance, and I woke up in the ER. The wreckage was huge. My first preference would have been to sweep it straight under the rug under my couch, dust my hands off on and carry on, I could not hide it. Our neighbors were curious,

Ryan's friend who was staying at our house that weekend, and our poor puppy were all concerned and confused. I woke up in the ER and through the fog that comes with overdosing, stomach pumping and trauma I realized I was still alive. I was furious—another failure. My mom was there consoling me, and I looked at her and said, "I thought you would be happy if I was gone." As a mother myself now, I know that destroyed her. The tears well up even now as I write this. What a horrible thing to say or think. I had no regard for life, not my own, not others, no one. The self-centeredness that had become my greatest character defect was never more evident than in that moment. What a shell of a monster I was.

Usually after a suicide attempt that lands you in the hospital, the next step is aftercare in a treatment facility with medication and therapy. But my life wasn't one of the usual sorts. I had a therapist. When Ryan contacted her, she was shocked to hear what I had done. She had no idea how much I was drinking or that I was suicidal—I didn't tell her the truth. I wasn't purposely lying; my perception didn't match reality. She was clueless. I told the doctors I was fine, that my suicide attempt was a cry for help. I was upset because of our fight and had been drinking too much, so I acted out. I must have been convincing because they sent me home with nothing but a prescription for Prozac. I was a master manipulator. For a long time, I was proud of that. I thought it meant I had power and control of myself. I fooled doctors and talked my way out of a mental institution. In recovery, I learned just how dysfunctional that was and how necessary learning empathy, compassion not only for others but for myself, and humility really are for the human spirit. There isn't a way to have peace and serenity and at the same time live a life of lies.

That was the last year of my drinking. I was miserable. By now everyone knew I drank too much, had a suicide attempt, and exercised obsessively. In the throes of a manic episode, I sanded off the textured ceiling of our powder room and painted a mural on the wall. I went out with my friends to bars on Friday nights for cheap beer. I would drink a few of those and still drive home. At another restaurant, I regularly ordered chips and salsa and a side salad for $5.00, just so I could have something in my stomach when I drank several draft beers. I had embarrassing moments at social events and got lectured by my mom about my behavior at Ryan's work functions. I would replace what I drank in our beer fridge to hide the amount I was consuming. I hid empty beer cans in my car and dumped them when I went to work. One memory I will never forget and can still sink my heart if I go there, is burned in my brain. From the window over our kitchen sink, I saw my husband taking the trash out behind our shed. I watched him look through the trash and saw his body slump down onto the trash can with what appeared to be complete defeat. He saw beer cans from one of my binges, and he couldn't believe what he saw. I knew that was my fault. The pain he was feeling in that moment, the disappointment was a direct result of my drinking, but it wasn't enough to stop it.

During graduate school, I created a delusion that I had to get straight A's. I was totally focused on that as well as trying to keep my body perfect, all while over-drinking daily. The sickness of addiction was pervasive and as I look back on that time now, I don't know how I even survived it. My thoughts were always negative and self-deprecating. I couldn't take a compliment. Toward the end of that year, my mental health problems started to catch up with me. I had trouble maintaining it all. I got my first B in grad school and was miserable. Failure. I was exhausted trying to keep up with the lies, the need to overwork, to be perfect. I had no self-love, no deep relationships; my spirit was crushed. I was a sad, scared little girl in my grown-up adult body. In the midst of that pain, I graduated in May 2002.

The following month, after the incident in Washington, D.C., my family as well as my lawyer believed it was best for me to go to rehab. I was totally clueless and had no experience with treatment centers. I hadn't known anyone who had been in one and had no idea what to expect. I arrived at this beautiful facility and immediately thought I didn't belong there. I was in the medical detox unit for three days and never unpacked a thing. I convinced myself that someone was going to come pick me up. I didn't think I belonged there. I continued that line of thinking for the first two weeks of my stay. I cried a lot, but no one came to my rescue. Despite my own perceptions of the reality that was called my life, I belonged there. We had visitation and Ryan came. When he left, I was devastated.

Once while in treatment I became incredibly upset. A wise counselor, an extremely tall, broad, black man who looked like an NFL player, came alongside me. He comforted me for a second and then said I needed to pull it together, that the other women were watching me. He told me I was a role model for them, that many of them didn't have visitors. He said I needed to focus on gratitude and strength. His message resonated with me, although I literally had no idea how I was a role model. His words helped me shift my emotional energy quickly. I was grateful for that man. He told stories and was kind to all of us. He would sit at the bottom of staircases and lovingly police us at night. I admired him, what he had been through and his recovery. He died from an overdose sometime after I was long gone from that place. The reality of addiction.

At that time, the main treatment modality was a twelve-step program. I didn't have the benefits of modern recovery with all the sobriety groups online and influencers writing profound memoirs with extensive research about the dangers of alcohol. The owner and namesake of the facility was Father Martin, an old priest who was an alcoholic himself. He sat in the cafeteria a couple times a week. Patients would tell him their stories, and he always had something wise to say. He shared his story, and we watched videos he had made about recovery. He was kind and compassionate and his legacy lives on for so many in recovery.

In rehab, there are no televisions anywhere. This is to remove you from your world and any distractions other than focusing on your recovery. There are no newspapers or magazines, and I couldn't talk to family members other than during specified phone and visitation times. I was stripped down to just me and my recovery. I hated it. I couldn't sit still, and I most certainly couldn't sit still in silence. There also wasn't any soda or sugar allowed, and I was addicted to diet soda. We had two hours of free time a day, and I spent almost all of that on the treadmill in the gym. I felt like I was going crazy. Because the problem was me. I used alcohol to self-soothe, to numb the feelings of anxiety, abandonment and loneliness. Take the alcohol away and I was left with all of that dysfunction and what seemed like no way to deal with it. I was scared of myself, of the feelings, and with no way to communicate about them to others, at least that's what I thought, the pressure just built with no release valve. I met some lovely women during my stay, they were supportive and relatable. I still communicate with some of them today.

The daily schedule in rehab is rigid. I learned to follow directions and be on a schedule, which is an important part of recovery. I had to relearn the basics of life from scratch. I got up at the same time in the morning, ate meals at the same times each day, brushed my teeth twice a day at the same times, and went to bed at the same time every night. The tasks that seem so elementary, but I had lost those abilities somewhere between leaving my parents' home and the time when I ended up in recovery.

We had group therapy, educational groups, and twelve-step meetings. There was limited free time, and we were expected to be at every meal and meeting. After I had been there for a couple weeks, they started taking us out into the community for twelve-step meetings. We rode on this cute little short-bus into town, and I remember wondering what the locals must have thought. "Oh, here come the crazy addicts."

I was thrilled to get out of the institutional environment and feel like I was part of society again. Occasionally we used this freedom to our advantage against the restrictions of the rehab. Once at a meeting next to a local fire department, we saw a soda machine in front of the building. A couple of us ladies planned ahead and brought some money. We asked people at the meeting to buy us as many diet sodas as we could afford, and we smuggled them back into the rehab. We laughed about it often, even years later. Here we were, people whose lives had been completely wrecked by drugs and alcohol, and we were now in rehab having to smuggle in diet soda.

I turned twenty-seven years old in rehab, which happened about two weeks in. I had spent those two weeks resisting the reality that was now my life. I was choosing not to connect with being in a treatment facility or identify with the other people there. I secretly prayed that my husband or parents would realize their mistake. On my birthday I sat outside overlooking the

Susquehanna River, and for the first time, I cried out to God. I surrendered and said, "I think maybe there is something wrong with my drinking. I need help." At that moment, I had my first spiritual awakening. The second two weeks were much different. I was involved, I participated, and I became willing to listen. During the last week of treatment, the facility hosted a family program. There was a lot of crying. I was grateful to have my network's back and to see their willingness to support me. Years of living with an active addict is sure to create quite a bit of dysfunction and a lot of feelings. I know now I could only grow and have healing in my family if I was willing to face the error of my ways and begin to build them as assets. In many ways, our dark past is the greatest passion we have and a profound key to relative happiness. I had spent years carrying too much of the past with me into my future. I also had trouble building friendships and allowing others in, because of my fear of being hurt. My time in rehab was the cracking open of a door. I was able to see love and connection on the other side. That made it worth it.

CHAPTER 6

PREPARATION IS THE KEY TO SUCCESS IN LIFE.

COMING HOME FROM REHAB WAS EXCITING, BUT also a little scary. We heard the statistics for addicts relapsing and it wasn't encouraging. I enrolled in an intensive outpatient program three nights a week. I went to Alcoholics Anonymous meetings, ninety meetings in ninety days. I felt better—a lot better. That's how it goes when you get sober. After thirty days you are as sober as you are ever going to get. The substances are gone from your physical body. You are no longer living in a cycle of thinking about the next drink, drinking, or nursing a hangover. It's possible you might have forgotten what that even feels like. You are sober, but you are now left with yourself and all the feelings.

There was an excitement around me. My husband and family were happy about this newfound journey, there was hope. It felt a lot like having a new baby. Everyone is very excited, there is joy and laughter and new toys and there is also a nervous energy. I am sure they were anxious as well. I went to meetings every day, and I started to meet other sober women. I liked the meetings—they were comforting like the weight of a heavy comforter. They felt safe; I belonged there even though it didn't truly feel like it yet. I still didn't quite believe I was an alcoholic. I was doing all these things because I wanted my husband to stay with me, I wanted to feel better, and frankly, I was too scared not to. But I didn't think I was an alcoholic. In fact, I remember writing that on the inside cover of my Alcoholics Anonymous book (The Big Book) and saying it to my sponsor several times. All they ever said was: "Keep coming back." It would take another eighteen months before I truly let go of the idea that I could drink like other people and was able to believe that I was an alcoholic.

I listened to people's stories during meetings and often I couldn't identify at all. I hadn't had the same experiences. Thankfully, someone told me to stop comparing stories and instead listen for the feelings. When I took out the events and listened to the desperation they shared, the powerlessness, the pain, I could relate to that for sure. I felt I was a high-functioning drunk; I hadn't experienced any devastating consequences. I had no DUIs, no loss of jobs, my husband didn't leave me, etc. I say that and at the same time think about the loss of myself in my addiction, the will to live. The time that was spent on drinking, thinking about drinking and cleaning up after the drinking. Managing the lies, covering up my actions, the destructive choices that hurt people I loved. Those seem like demoralizing consequences but were boiled down and glossed over because they didn't involve major socially unacceptable problems like jail time, homelessness, or unemployment. Except for the one time I was arrested. I was blessed to be welcomed back to that job for the state even after what I had been through. Later I was told by my sponsor when we were doing my fifth step work that my list of transgressions wasn't long but what I had on there was monumental.

Someone in rehab suggested that I find a sponsor and go to AA meetings every day for at least ninety days and then beyond. I did that because I was willing to do whatever it took to get better. I attended meetings in my area during lunch, and they were helpful. I met many women and learned something new with every meeting. I found a homegroup (a meeting you claim as your home base, attend every week, and volunteer to help) on Monday nights in a candlelit church basement sitting at round tables with twenty or thirty other alcoholics trying to find their way. There were all kinds of people there, young and old. I didn't believe I really belonged there, since I was in denial that I was an alcoholic. And I also found incredible peace and excitement in those rooms. I couldn't sit still in meetings. I was fidgety and if asked to read, I spoke so fast that it was hard to understand me. I heard the stories, the emotions, the desperation of those other sick and suffering people. Although no one had my exact story, I could relate to the feelings they shared.

I struggled much of my life in building relationships with other women, as I found them to be judgmental, fake, and rarely trustworthy. I didn't really think they understood me. In AA you are advised to stick with your own gender when selecting a sponsor. I got phone numbers and had coffee with a few women that I had met in meetings. Picking a sponsor seemed like the most challenging obstacle ever. Who would understand me? Who would be able to handle me? I was nervous about sharing my story and feelings with someone new, a complete stranger. This is laughable because the people you are sharing with are recovering alcoholics, likely with similar experiences if not much worse. Thankfully, God sent just the right one. In the late 1990s and 2000s, there was a popular company called Longaberger Baskets. It was a multilevel marketing brand that sold these expensive specialty baskets in all shapes and sizes and functions. They were extremely popular. I had hosted many parties and owned a variety of baskets. When I got to AA and saw a woman carrying a Longaberger Basket purse, I knew she was my people. I didn't know Betsy but quickly found my way over to introduce myself. Because of that purse, I asked her to be my sponsor. That's where I was at the time.

That relationship led me to learn more about what it meant to be a member of AA and work the steps. This woman was gentle, kind, and compassionate. She cared deeply about me and my healing, as well as her own sobriety. As a woman who struggled with connections and didn't feel I had any value at all, this was astonishing to me. I had trouble accepting her love and support and was keeping a close watch for betrayal, disappointment and abandonment. It didn't come.

Betsy had been raised in AA by strong sober alcoholics well versed in the Big Book and the program of Alcoholics Anonymous. She told me to carry a Big Book around with me, that it would keep the crazies away. She's the one who taught me not to compare stories during meetings, but instead to listen for the feelings. So, when the old men of AA in my community were sharing about losing jobs, houses, wives and jail time I learned not to check out. I heard them talk about feeling different than their fellows, the loneliness and desperation they felt. I heard their pain. Our stories are unique to us of course. That will always be true, and I could usually find plenty of people to point to that would back that up. But the emotions of someone living in addiction are a shared experience. Those feelings give rise to water-cooler moments when you realize you aren't alone. Someone else has experienced the mental anguish and torture that we used substances to escape from. That lends itself to deep personal connection despite being quite different in every other way. I can't think of another space in life where this is the case.

I learned from Betsy how to work the steps of recovery, why they were supposed to be done in order, and why I should continue going to meetings. She was a breath of fresh air and truly met me right at my level of need. Betsy introduced me to other women in the program, and I started going to a Big Book study group in one of their homes. It was awesome because she cooked for us every week, and it was a more intimate environment than the regular meetings. I learned so much from those women. Not only about being an alcoholic and recovering, but also about how to be a friend. They were open and honest in their sharing. All of them genuinely wanted to develop stronger relationships. This felt refreshing and scary at the same time. I was eager to share parts of me but also struggled with vulnerability. It is hard getting honest about yourself, your feelings and your actions with other people.

Betsy taught me about creating healthy routines and discipline. She told me to pray every morning and ask my higher power to guide me according to his will. And then at night say thank you for helping me stay sober today. She told me to call her every single day, go to meetings, and read my Big Book. I didn't really understand it at the time, but I did all those things. Creating discipline is a huge part of building a life in recovery and something I thought I already had. But it was important for me to learn how to follow directions. I started taking care of myself better. My daily hygiene improved, I was eating healthier and exercising regularly. Other people in my life started to notice. They would comment that I was laughing more. I can't say enough about the importance of a sponsor relationship in early sobriety. Whether you like twelve-step programs or not, there is a benefit of having the fellowship and support rise up around you rather than trying to navigate recovery on your own. There is too much going on. I'm certain it can be done, but it is a lot easier, and you are more likely to succeed with the help of others. It worked for me.

For me, AA was easy. I liked it because I felt like I belonged for the first time in my life. I couldn't believe the honesty with which people shared their experience and how we could laugh at some of the most horrific experiences. Nowhere else can you honestly share your feelings, mistakes, tragedies, and successes in the way that you can in AA. I instantly had people to talk to who had similar feelings. AA met me right where I was, and I stayed sober. I was taught early on that AA isn't the only way to get sober. It was the way I knew. AA gave me the preparation I needed to function and survive without drinking. The steps, the sponsor, the meetings were all what led me to success in recovery.

CHAPTER 7

JUST BECAUSE I AM SOBER
DOESN'T MEAN I AM WELL.

WHEN I WAS SIX MONTHS SOBER, I GOT pregnant for the first time. I was twenty-seven years old, and I was anxious to have children. I felt the time was passing quickly like the minutes on a clock during vacation. Ryan and I were ecstatic to learn we would be parents in October 2003. We read the books, took the prenatal classes, went to doctors' appointments, and we waited to find out the sex of our baby. The whole family was excited as this was the first grandchild on both sides. There were showers and gifts, and Ryan built the most amazing nursery in our home. At meetings everyone doted on me and my growing belly. I continued step work and meetings, but the pregnancy gave me something fresh to focus on. I wasn't thinking about not drinking much because now I really couldn't. There were doubts and fears, but mostly it was excitement and learning everything I could about labor and delivery and raising an infant. I wrote a five-page birth plan with all my desires including: no medication (that didn't work out), no pacifiers, and no nurseries for my baby. Perfectionism meets pregnancy and motherhood.

The joy we had when our firstborn daughter came into our lives is indescribable. Grace was perfect, stunningly gorgeous with luscious black waves in her hair, and she was a great baby. Like many mothers and babies, especially the first time, we struggled with nursing. She wasn't getting quite enough calories, she lost some weight and was jaundiced, so she spent a couple nights in the nursery while we went home. At the time it felt like the most gut-wrenching pain to leave her at the hospital, even though I knew she was where she needed to be. I pumped breastmilk several times a day, took the milk to the hospital, and rocked her for hours. She came home after two days and has been healthy ever since.

Sometime after having this perfect first baby, I received a letter from my biological father. In the letter, he acknowledged that I had a baby and suggested we get together. He also indicated his love for me in his own way as a sort of amends. It was an olive branch. It had been six or seven years since we had spoken or seen each other. There were a lot of emotions, and I was still early in recovery. I was shocked to hear from him, especially after such a long period of silence between us. I felt angry. Did he really think we were going to sit around a family table together? I also felt so much confusion about this person. Was I supposed to want to have a relationship with him? Was it wrong to cut him out of my life? Were my perceptions about our history unrealistic? It felt like an emotional gut punch. I was worried what my parents would think. How would they feel if I considered opening the door to him now, and not only for me but for Grace and possibly any children I had after this? I believed they would feel betrayed.

The mama bear in me came out immediately and all I could think was HELL NO, this man does not get to have access to this baby or me. When I was younger, I couldn't protect myself from him, I couldn't stop the abandonment or the deep scars he left when we called him over and over and he wouldn't pick up. Now I could protect Grace as well as myself from that dysfunctional relationship. Thankfully, I had a program of recovery in my life to help me work through this in a healthy way, so I didn't do something immature and make an ass of myself. I spent time with my sponsor talking about these feelings. I was upset, angry, frustrated, and found myself asking "why?". Together we formulated a plan that worked for me. I wrote a letter back, had my sponsor read through it, and sent it. I wrote that it was my job to protect this child from the emotional turmoil of loved ones coming in and out of her life. There didn't seem to be any reason to expose her to that level of pain. I sent it and never heard back.

I was proud of myself for taking a stand. I had been

through him deciding to come into my life and just as quickly fading back out. Grace was my child, and I had the ability to decide what was best for her and who was best for her. I knew there would come a time when she was older and would learn about our family history. She would know that her grandfather was not her biological grandfather, and I was prepared to deal with that when the time came. I wasn't trying to keep it a secret. There was no evidence to support my biological father wanting to have a sustained relationship with me or my family. That doesn't make him a bad person (I learned that in therapy), but it does make him someone that wasn't good for me and not such a great dad. Being in recovery made this realization and distinction possible. When I was drinking, I would not have been able to process that experience in a healthy way. I went to meetings. I continued working the steps. I prayed about it. I felt the discomfort, allowed the feelings to come in and out, and I didn't drink. I learned some people are not for us, even the ones that seem like they should be. By doing a lot of personal work and growth what I know is my father was not capable of loving in a normal way. He was likely an alcoholic. We found out years later when he died that his affairs had been less than in order. He was a reckless man, irresponsible and without the ability to connect emotionally. His cold alcoholic upbringing likely left him with untreated trauma, and the cycle continued with us.

I loved the entire experience of being pregnant and having a baby and couldn't wait to do it again.

Nine months after Grace was born, we were pregnant again. I brought Grace to meetings with me in her carrier and everyone loved it. Nothing like a baby to bring a community together. While we waited for baby #2, Grace and I had special time together. She was with both grandmothers while I worked part-time. The love that was given her, the pictures, the spoiling, it was all incredibly special. Her first Christmas dress that I still have in a memory box and the pictures with her full head of dark baby curls are burned in my memory forever.

I had the same experience with my second pregnancy, labor, and delivery. It was beautiful. We did not learn the sex of this child either and were surprised by another girl. Baby Nora was born in April 2005. She was just as perfect as her sister, but a little noisier. The nursing and care for Nora were a bit easier, plus, I had more confidence about what I was doing. However, bringing a second baby home is still a challenge. It added quite a bit of stress and as is so often the case for parents with young children, it began challenging our marriage. Thankfully, I was able to work two and a half days a week after Grace was born. Both grandmothers were helping with childcare but adding the second baby so soon was tough for everyone. The grandmothers continued to watch the babies, but they were challenged, too. We did our best, but I remember the strain that became apparent as we worked through the daily struggles of parenting littles. It was harder to leave two babies home at night to go to meetings. I still went, but not every day. I still worked with my sponsor and was connected to a group.

I remember some of the old-timers saying things like "meeting makers make it," "it works if you work it," and "anything you put before your sobriety you will lose." It felt stressful trying to juggle everything. My sponsor was wise, and a mother. She told me I got sober to live my life not for AA to become my life. That was helpful. She wasn't saying not to attend meetings or work a program but was suggesting that being of service to my family was part of my program. I could read the Big Book, listen to stories on CD, and call people. I am grateful I was being led by women in AA like her, otherwise, I am not sure what would have happened. It's possible I would have burnt out on recovery, neglected my husband and children for AA, or become resentful of one or both.

Soon after Nora's birth, I started therapy with a phenomenal and well-known EMDR therapist in our area. She was known in the recovery community as the go-to person for outside help. EMDR or Eye Movement Desensitization and Reprocessing is a specialized and neurologically based form of trauma treatment that is used to reprocess old and disturbing events from our lives and reframe them in a more positive way. Basically, it cleanses the brain of the negative beliefs you have about yourself that form from unprocessed trauma throughout your life. It is the closest thing we have to a miracle for healing the brain from the damage that trauma does, even trauma that happens early in life. The process began. Together we started to lay out the events of my life going back as far as I could remember that helped to create my negative beliefs about myself, my perception problems, and ultimately addiction. Most of our work focused on early childhood trauma from my father leaving our family and abandoning us. I remember wondering what was wrong with me. I don't have any of the big traumas. I wasn't sexually abused, I wasn't neglected, I was raised in a loving family with everything I needed and most things I wanted. It felt as though I was being a whiny baby talking about my feelings of not being good enough and feeling like a failure. I struggled with that for a long time.

Thank goodness for therapy, because trauma is relative. What I experience as being painful or leaving a mark on my brain might be nothing to someone else, and vice versa. I didn't understand that until much later, as I built my own therapy practice. So often, as children depending on personality, familial circumstances, and environment, we internalize events around us and our perceptions become our reality. When substances are added into the mix, things get jumbled up even more and the distortions grow and change. Every child in every family perceives situations in their own way. Other children raised by the same parents have different experiences within the same family. Differing factors include school, learning differences, friends, intimate relationships, and work experiences. We are all different on multiple levels. Comparing our insides to what we see on the outsides of others never works.

Ryan and I were working, raising our beautiful girls, taking them to church, preschool, and mommy-and-me gymnastics. I was trying to maintain some level of a recovery program in my life. I was relatively happy at that time, loved being a mom, and was sober. There was, however, a bit of discontentment. I still didn't have many of the emotional sobriety tools necessary to live my best life. I struggled in my marriage to speak up for my own needs. I just didn't have the confidence I needed for that, partly because I didn't totally feel worthy of even having needs. I allowed myself to be a bit of a doormat because of this, and shifting that energy took effort. I don't think I was capable of articulating any of that at the time. Looking back, I can easily point out my flaws and missteps along the way.

I was intently focused on raising healthy kids. I didn't conform to the mainstream advice in child rearing, I was drawn more to the natural approach in most areas. I made my own baby food, nursed them for thirteen months each, and they never had formula or pacifiers. They definitely didn't have sugar or juice or gummies. And as a result, they thrived in their early years. That was my focus. I was passionate about living a healthy lifestyle and showing my kids a great example. Sometimes getting the grandparents on board was challenging, but I know they appreciated our efforts to keep the girls as healthy as possible.

I knew after I had Nora that our family wasn't complete; I longed for another child. The transition from one child to two children still stung a bit as we settled into life with kids who were eighteen months apart. Eventually I became pregnant for the last time. With a third baby on the way, we knew it was time for me to stay home with them full time. Daycare would then become more than I was even bringing home, plus I wanted to be with our kids. Daycare just didn't make sense anymore. Thankfully, I was able to finish the supervision hours necessary to take my licensure exam and become a Licensed Clinical Social Worker before I left my job with the state. A decision that would be incredibly valuable later in my life.

When Nora was two and a half, we brought home our third child, our son, Derek. He was the biggest one yet at ten pounds. Everyone was excited, and I knew our family was complete. That was three kids in four years, and I had been sober for five. We really knew how to pack a bunch of life into a short time. After having two kids, the third felt like a breeze. He got toted around to his sisters' activities, rode in the carrier and stroller, and slept better. Grace and Nora were in preschool, which gave us a place to go every day. The preschool was inside our gym. We dropped them off each morning, then Derek went to the nursery, and I worked out. That gym was a life-saver. That was where I often chased friendships with what I call "the beautiful people." The women in the 9:00-11:00 a.m. gym crowd were much different from those in the after 5:00 p.m. crew. They were dressed in designer workout clothes, their kids were well behaved and in matching outfits, they wore lipstick, and had beautifully manicured hair and nails. I was friends with many of them. In fact, I worked hard to get "in" with them for years. I was a bit of a misfit. I didn't really have my shit together. Although we made it there every day, usually on time or early, I was often in tears as I pushed that double stroller through the automatic doors. I don't know why, things just felt harder for me. We were not the same.

Those years reignited my "I'm not good enough" negative beliefs. I was the mom that wanted to be honest, to share the real stuff of parenting and marriage, really connect on a more intimate level with other women. I quickly learned not to cross that line. I remember sharing what I thought were common struggles related to raising young kids and seeing nothing but a glassy-eyed stare in return. Some even said, "No that's never happened to me," or "Oh gosh, I can't relate to that." It reinforced my perception that my life was not in order, I was a hot mess, and most women were doing all this much better than I was. Behind closed doors lived the reality of their own lives, likely different from what they showed in the preschool drop-off line. I wanted a more vulnerable connection with my friends, a realness that wasn't accessible in this crowd. I was relentless. I just kept pushing and trying, since our kids were friends. There were many red flags along the way. It was like being a teenage girl again, trying to fit in with the popular crowd but inside knowing that I didn't fit in. It reminds me of the scene in the movie *Apollo 13* when the engineers discover they are having a problem with carbon dioxide buildup due to the length of time they were in space. But the filters they need are round and the only options they have on the aircraft to use are square. The head engineer says, "well I suggest you gentlemen invent a way to put a square peg in a round hole, rapidly". Although in this case human ingenuity to create the solution for this is nothing short of miraculous, doing this in my social life represents the definition of insanity. What a waste of time. If I could go back now, I would have put more effort into finding authentic relationships that were aligned with my own values. I would have spent more time getting to know my own children, playing with them, communicating more deeply. It always seems easier when we are looking back. Now raising teenagers, I find myself telling them not to do as I did. Find the people that really matter, the ones that get you and accept you. Go to the gym with the evening crowd.

I believe now that I missed out on forming lasting relationships with other women in my community that I could be doing life with today. I felt different from those women, similar to how I felt when I was younger or during my drinking. It was a serious realization but also awkward because I actually WAS different. I didn't drink. I had this thing, this part of me that was dramatically obvious and seemingly a flaw. Something that needed explaining or so I thought. I never wanted to drink again. I knew I had way too much to lose. I wanted to be accepted as myself, with all my flaws and mistakes and hot-mess days. Acceptance also included relatability which wasn't there in that crowd.

I needed connection. I needed to share my truth with other women. I needed to be known and seen. I needed to tell someone that just because I was sober, that did not mean that I was well.

CHAPTER 8

MOST OF THE STORIES WE TELL OURSELVES ARE NOT TRUE.

A T FOUR YEARS INTO RECOVERY, I HAD MY FIRST sober bottom. Life was full, chaotic, blessed, but also lonely. I was deeply rooted in the AA community, had a homegroup, had a sponsor, and went to meetings. With all of that in place, I still couldn't find women who were like me. There were no young moms in the rooms at that time, at least not in my area. There wasn't Facebook nor any online spaces for women in recovery. It was different from the modern sober woman's experience. Even though I had a lot of friends, the authenticity factor was missing. The friends I did make moved away and the connection faded. The progress that occurred through working a recovery program was profound. Through my use of tools like acceptance, forgiveness, and prayer, I grew emotionally. I changed. With these tools and continued support in recovery and therapy, the I'm-not-good-enough negative belief was slowly squashed. The daily effort put into a morning meditation routine, focusing on gratitude, and viewing my role as a mother as a service to my family led me to peace and serenity in my mind and body that I had never known before. There came a time when I finally realized the women I was trying to be "in" with weren't my people. They weren't bad people by any means; they had great lives and families. They just weren't for me.

Unfortunately, the insidious nature of discontentment began to build inside of me. I didn't know where I fit in. I was parenting three littles, and sober. My life was full and good from the outside looking in. Many would kill to have what I had. We were blessed. My husband worked hard, was a great provider and a supportive partner. I was the CEO of our family: planning, driving, entertaining, and feeding everyone. We did major renovations to our home, and I was the project manager. The kids went to preschool, gymnastics, soccer, and dance. We worked out regularly and ate healthfully. Something still wasn't quite right. I began to pull away gradually from my recovery regimen. Meetings were still part of my life but less so. I wasn't actively working the steps or communicating with my sponsor. My connection with my higher power began to wane as I turned my back on the God I knew and loved. It's almost like I was internally having an adult tantrum. I knew the things I was supposed to do, but I just wasn't doing them. I was busy. My husband and I needed time together at night. I resented the lack of connection with my husband, my God, and my spiritual community. I wasn't spiritually fit. In those earlier years, this was almost always because of unrealistic expectations. Instead of using the tools I knew would work, I kept on going, kept pushing forward, but I did not talk about it.

There wasn't a specific incident or issue I could point to and blame for this time. Just the perfect storm of not taking care of myself properly and the demands of a beautiful and blessed life. I believe the lack of a true recovery community, meaning one I was vulnerable and raw with, was a huge factor. I did not blame anyone for this. Just because I couldn't find women similar to me at the two meetings I attended regularly, didn't mean they weren't out there. Maybe I should have gotten a little more involved. I was gradually becoming the woman who was around AA but not in it. This caused just enough distance to create a struggle. The emotional sobriety wasn't there. I was sober but not much better than a dry drunk.

I used to share about this time a lot in meetings. No one ever told me this could happen in sobriety. I hadn't heard others talk about how they felt similar to how they did at the end of their drinking but without picking up a drink. I heard people say, "Meeting makers make it," and "It works if you work it." In my view from the chair in twelve-step meetings, I was doing those things. It just wasn't enough and that translated into I wasn't enough. AA couldn't meet me at my level of need at that time because I needed more. I needed a new and improved toolbox for this stage of life. I needed support in becoming a more mature wife and mother, someone that could speak up for herself and be content in her life. I needed a swift kick in the butt. To take personal responsibility for my life, feelings, and actions. I needed to stop looking for external validation. The culmination of this period for me, was sometime that year when I found myself standing on the back porch of my house crying. I was desperate for something, someone, anything to help me. I cried out to my God and said, "I need help." I believe this was my second formal surrender and spiritual awakening. I called my sponsor and told her I needed help. That something was wrong with me. I didn't know what to do or how to fix it. I didn't want to drink, but I didn't want to live that way either.

She said, "I've been waiting for you, welcome back". Like every time before and since, AA and the recovery community met me right where I was with open arms and big warm smiles. I realized it was me that was disconnected. I wasn't doing the things I needed to do to stay emotionally well. So, I got busy in the program, worked with my sponsor on some step work and followed directions. I also went back to therapy to do more healing work. Ryan and I made a more conscious effort with date nights and some therapy, too. I decided to go back to work one day a week for a while, just to use my brain and learn the clinical skills I needed to become a stronger therapist. We hired a babysitter for one day a week. I started receiving acupuncture regularly and eventually running longer distances. I was building the tools to support a life I didn't want to escape from and become not only mentally tough but also at peace on the inside.

This growth period was a work in progress, not an overnight phenomenon. Out of that time came a beautiful transformation. I realized that the stories I had told myself just were not true. I found clarity around my own needs, and a strength emerged to carry on with my life despite the challenges that kept coming. The other side of the pain and overwhelm was better. All my problems did not get solved, but I was better.

CHAPTER 9

THERE IS A GOD AND I'M NOT HIM (THANK GOD).

BUILDING A FAMILY AND RAISING CHILDREN IN recovery was a test for me. It was also the biggest blessing I have experienced. Everything from preschool drama and sleep problems, transitioning to kindergarten, spending tons of weekends in Deep Creek Lake with family in the winter going skiing and enjoying summers on the boat and outdoors. We vacationed together in the summer, Ryan spent Saturday mornings at his parent's home for breakfast while I went to a meeting, and we all attended sporting events, school concerts, and parties. We went to church and Sunday School, and there were many Sunday family dinners.

We had challenges with our children along the way. After a few incidents where we felt the large public school system was not serving the girls the way we would prefer, we made the decision to move them to a much smaller, private, classical Christian School. Making the decision to move them wasn't hard, as I had always had the dream of sending them to a smaller, Christian-based school. I viewed it as an opportunity to be supported by the school in our parenting. To have help in shaping their hearts and character. The day I took our application to New Covenant Christian School with a check for tuition, I felt doubt and fear rise up inside of me. In that moment, the uncertainty became overwhelming. I was questioning our decision-making. Was this the right thing? Was this school the right place?

During this time, I attended a meeting in a wise woman's home. She taught me the three R's, which apply in many situations: Refrain, Reflect, and Respond. She had a million years of sobriety and was amazing at leading other women through the recovery process. She opened her home and made dinner for us, and free homemade food was extremely appealing to me. I remember going there every week and feeling so comfortable, so cared for; I fit in. This was nothing like the experience I had with women in other periods of my life. Never had I found a space where I could share the truth of my experience and not get looks of shock in return. And with women who in general I likely wouldn't have encountered because our lives were quite different. I learned things like the three R's and how to allow other women to care about me. I could tell I was still guarded but much more open than in the past. I liked it. I was worthy of their love.

In the New Covenant parking lot, I recalled the three Rs. First, I slowed myself down (Refrain) and went through the decision once again. I carefully reviewed the reasons we had discussed so many times for making this significant change. I asked myself, "what am I doing this for". The answers were clearer to me than ever. When we are faced with decisions, taking our time can be one of the best things we do. I was considering all the points (Reflect). I knew the arguments against doing it. I had heard them all and run through scenarios in my head over and over. I also knew the type of family we were. Our kids were heavily involved in their community through sports, church, and family. They weren't isolated. The benefits of this school certainly outweighed any consequences I could even imagine. I prayed before I walked in the building that God would guide and direct our steps with the children, for they don't belong to us after all. This careful discernment for just a few moments gave me the confidence and strength I needed to properly respond to what felt like a major life changing event.

I walked in the building (Respond) and started crying as I handed off the application to the woman behind the desk. She extended a type of kindness I don't know that I have received in any other place. She even said if you don't think this is the right fit or the right time it can wait. I told her that wasn't it at all. I knew in my heart it was the best decision for us and the tears were more an indication of letting go of the overwhelm, allowing God to be my director, and an acceptance of change.

The three R's is a back pocket tool I pull out almost daily to work through decisions and emotions. It has become foundational for me. Often, I have self-doubt, based on the opinions of other people in my life or from the world. The doubt I was having about this seemingly huge school decision for my children was fueled somewhat by my perception of other people's opinions. But when I slowed myself down to allow my mind to clear, the emotions to settle, to listen for the voice of God, I was able to respond properly. There was a draw to this school for our children. The kind that was undeniable. The kind when you are pulled towards something or someone in a divine way with the strength of angels. The moment we walked into the school building for the first time for a visit I knew. My heart was filled with what I can only describe as the loving hand of God, and it felt completely right. The teachers instructing the students with loving firmness, the moral code and character development, the expectations and accountability, and the stellar curriculum were all there. I knew my children would have opportunities in learning that I never had. They would get to see examples of people who loved God and could defend their worldview. The manners and respect the children displayed were like nothing I had ever seen. They even wore uniforms, making it easier on the kids and us.

After a period without a strong relationship with

a sponsor and without a strong connection to the program, I celebrated my ten-year anniversary. I switched home groups after about eight years of sobriety. My kids were school-age now and keeping me busy with their extra-curricular activities, so my involvement in AA was becoming less frequent. The old-timers would make comments about not seeing me for a while or how anything you put before your sobriety you will lose. I remembered what I was taught about living my life rather than making AA my life. I experienced no desire to drink. I had also done the trauma work, was utilizing acupuncture, exercising regularly, and hired babysitters when I needed help.

We started having struggles with Grace when she was in second grade. Her behavior challenges were part of the reason we changed schools. We wanted a school that provided a smaller, more supportive environment. The school did not disappoint. As parents, we had to work through the emotional parts of how her behavior affected our family. That process created some marital challenges as well. Although we were usually on the same page with discipline and the need for intervention, we experienced doubt within ourselves about our parenting decisions. We asked ourselves, "What did we did wrong? What are we doing wrong now?" We turned on each other. This was difficult, and I struggled to find the type of support system in which I could be open and honest. I was missing deeper connections with friends.

I was always a deeply social person; I craved connection with others, adventure, and gatherings. Ryan and I developed some good friendships through our kids' activities, and we spent a lot of time with our family. The loneliness was still ever present for me. I didn't know who I could trust with my story, with my kids' stories, with my life. I had experienced the consequences that can come from those who don't understand and don't keep your confidence. I didn't have the tribe some women rave about. Looking back through my life, that has been a missing link. I learned to live life while holding myself back, but it felt fake. Being a mom, or at least the kind I wanted to be, required almost all my time and attention. Showing up for my kids and providing a home that was comfortable, warm, and loving was no easy task; it was a lot of work.

Hearing the stories of those women who were still drinking while they were parenting was always a great reminder for me of how blessed I was. I didn't have all the wreckage they did when it came to my children. I didn't have to make amends to them for horrific events or for being checked out. My kids never had to worry about inviting their friends over, if mom could drive them somewhere, or if their parents would be engaged in a brutal battle. They were privileged in growing up in a sober home. For many years, Ryan didn't even drink as a way of showing his support for me. We didn't have alcohol in our home, so our kids only saw it with other family members or when we were out socially. For that, I am incredibly grateful. I have seen the damage other moms have done and the unforgiving pain they experienced because of the things they have done or said. That's what addiction does to families.

When my oldest daughter was in third grade, it was her first year in the new school. One of the reasons we chose this school was because of its Christian teaching and intense character development. They operated with a loving firmness that was so attractive to us as parents, and you could tell that was having a profound effect on the students. Grace had been struggling with some behavior challenges the year before, and we were just beginning to get a handle on those. She was seeing a therapist, we were working together as a family, and with the school. She was friendly, outgoing, talkative, and fun; however, she also was a bit of an attention seeker. Grace would lie about things in her life. We believed she was trying to make herself look more desirable as a friend. She also tended to latch on to one friend and leave her boundaries in the wind.

Third grade tends to be a big transition year for kids. They are starting to become more independent thinkers, and they are identifying those friends they feel most comfortable with. At that age, they gravitate more to friends they actually like versus being friends with the whole class. Of course, this mirrors real life in many ways, as most adults don't naturally gravitate to everyone in their work environment or everyone in a social situation. We tend to stick with the people we have common interests with and who have similar energy. Grace was friendly with all the girls in her class but was particularly close with one of the girls. However, there was some conflict building between Grace and another girl in the class. I honestly can't really remember the details of the conflict. Over time we became aware that Grace and this other girl weren't really getting along. The conflict escalated, the other girl's parents reached out to the administration, and the school became involved. The parents of this child were concerned about the way Grace was treating their daughter. The principal at the school suggested we have a meeting with both sets of parents as well as the teacher to talk about what was going on and to devise a solution. Ryan and I discussed this, and we both had reservations about the meeting. I also discussed it with my sponsor, who had been down this road before. She basically said that we should not attend the meeting with the other parents being present. We decided we would go through with the meeting despite that advice. So I sought my sponsor's counsel again to decide how best to handle ourselves. I was going to need a plan and some serious strategies before going into that room. Even though we were going against her advice, I was still looking for guidance in how to handle this situation in the best possible way and I knew she had experiences with her own children that would help inform us in a positive way.

My sponsor suggested if we were to have the meeting, that we should sit there and listen, say little or nothing at all, and see how things go. I liked that suggestion as I am a firm believer in listening more than I speak in most situations. But I also know we were going to walk the walk, defend, justify, share anything we felt necessary because we love our daughter. The morning of the meeting I woke up with the heaviness of dread, my stomach was in knots. I had no idea what to expect. We didn't know these parents, and anytime your child is on the chopping block it is nerve-wracking. Ryan and I went to the principal's office where we were joined by the other two parents and the third-grade teacher. The principal was an older woman who had been with the school for many years. She was a "typical" church lady if ever there was one. Grey hair, heavyset, soft-spoken, loving eyes that said, "Welcome, come into my world." She was a kind and loving woman who tended to coddle the children. She had been known to "scold" a youngster with a strong talking to and send them back to class with a sticker. In the conversation we had with her originally about the meeting, she indicated that she wanted to bring us all together because she wanted the parents at her school to be friends. That was not our goal. At this point in our lives, we had well-established social circles, I had three kids, a growing business, my husband worked a lot, and honestly, we weren't really interested in forcing new friendships with couples at our kids' new school.

We sat down across the desk in an office that was much too small for six people, and the meeting began. Before I walked into the building I had prayed because that is what I had been taught to do when I got sober. I asked God to guide and direct my steps and my words according to His will. I prayed that everyone involved would have the kids' wellbeing as their goal, and we could come to a resolution for all. I did this because praying and grounding myself became a life skill I used anytime I was going into a challenging situation. I was taught to fix my eyes on an energy source outside myself and put out to that source what I wished to receive back. I already had a strong belief in God as my higher power, so this concept wasn't unfamiliar. I know that isn't the same for everyone who gets sober, and that's ok. We come from different places; we have had different experiences, some of which are traumatic. The important thing in any recovery journey is to become willing to connect and harness the energy from a source outside yourself, whatever that is. Inevitably, self-reliance will fail us. Following directions is often not our natural way, it is a learned response after we get and stay sober. So, I did what I was taught to do and prayed before I went in. My heart was racing, my stomach was queasy, but I kept hearing My sponsor's voice. "Don't say anything." I shared that with Ryan before we went in, so we were in agreement. The principal started off the meeting with her usual pleasantries, recounting why she asked us to come together and then turned it over to us. The third-grade teacher shared her summary of the conflict between the girls quickly and seemed unphased by all of it. The mother of the other child pulled out a pad with a long list of grievances against Grace and began listing them. I know the word bully was used more than once. For forty-five minutes, my husband and I sat next to each other in a tiny principal's office while another set of parents shared all the reasons they believed their daughter was being harmed by ours. That was one of the most difficult things I had ever endured since becoming a mom. After some time, the teacher got up and left, visibly annoyed by the situation. Towards the end, Ryan started to make a motion like he was going to say something. I put my hand on his leg and gave him a gentle squeeze to stop him. Say nothing.

Eventually it ended. There was some discussion about keeping the girls separated from each other (in a school with one class per grade and a class size of fifteen) and moving past this situation. I had a bit of a meltdown after we left but also a sense of relief and almost pride because we didn't fight back, we weren't aggressive, defensive, or threatening. We took it. It was hard, but we took it. I had followed the guidance from another sober woman on how to conduct myself in this challenging situation. I didn't have to drink over it, and I didn't die. The next day I was in the school to volunteer for something and that third-grade teacher, a special woman in my book, pulled me aside and said "I know that was really hard what you did yesterday. But you did exactly the right thing." I let out a huge sigh of relief and started to tear up. I never would have expected to get this kind of validation but there it was. Confirmation that we had shown up for our kid, advocated for her even, without saying a word. She ended the conversation by saying, "Some people are just really difficult." And there it was, just the tidbit I needed to know that this wasn't about us. This wasn't about my daughter being a bully or her lying or a desire to be seen by other girls, accepted, and loved. This was about them.

The difficult situations of life will come. We don't have to go out and look for them, put an ad on a billboard or ask; nope they will fall right into our laps without us moving a muscle. And in active addiction it was easier because we weren't present in our own lives, we weren't feeling the hard feelings that come from life. We made every excuse we could and poured substances of any kind into our bodies just so we didn't have to deal with the discomfort of difficult people, pain, or grief. And when you take away the drink and the drug, you are left with nothing. You are completely raw and exposed like an open wound. The salt from living gets poured on and rubbed in unless you put practices, tools, and people into your life to replace the substance. If I hadn't done that, if I hadn't listened to what people were teaching me, there is no way I would have been able to deal with that meeting about Grace. And I wouldn't have stayed sober.

Even though there were struggles with kids or family members, parenting younger children was delightful in many ways. I loved being up at the school volunteering, driving for field trips, and managing play dates. Ryan had a great job and was climbing the corporate ladder. He was a super hard worker but always was there for the kids. I was running our household, but every time I needed something he was there. Sobriety was good. I was relatively happy. I struggled sometimes with overwhelm and found myself spinning my wheels with all the tasks to do. I don't think I intuitively knew how to handle some situations. I often felt alone and as if I didn't know what to do. I know today I was never alone. I am so thankful for the guidance and wisdom of God. He guided me out of addiction before I knew I wanted out. He provided the relationships I needed when I needed them. Trying to do sobriety and recovery on my own did not work. I was only successful to the extent that I consistently surrendered to the will of God.

CHAPTER 10

GOD AND I ARE THE ONLY ONES WHO CAN TAKE CARE OF ME

AS THE KIDS GOT OLDER AND MY YOUNGEST WAS getting closer to going off to kindergarten, I started to feel the pull to get back to work outside of our home. I knew I had to remain flexible with a schedule I could control, since we were driving kids to and from school every day. Ryan was working a lot and traveling more. The logical answer was to create a private practice and start doing therapy. I had no idea how to do that, but I knew that was my best bet at making extra money while rebuilding my career. I had zero experience starting a business or even working in business, as I was coming out of government service. Thankfully, my husband became my business manager, and we worked together to get my practice up and running. I spent hours poring over the insurance panel credentialing process. I remember sitting in Starbucks while my son was at preschool and filling out all these papers. By the time he went off to kindergarten in September 2013, I had rented an office, decorated it, and was marketing myself.

Those old tapes of self-doubt were playing inside of me, but now at a lower frequency. I now had the confidence that stemmed from years of recovery work, the program of Alcoholics Anonymous, and the support of my husband. I had fun making that office my own. I picked out just the right shade of taupe to make it feel comfortable and spa-like. I bought inviting furniture, fake plants, and beautiful light fixtures. I couldn't believe this was my office. It was shocking to me. I had dreams of being a health coach, using my passion for health and wellness to help change the lives of others using their own bodies. Most of me was in denial about being a therapist. I didn't feel that was my role, or that I had the clinical skills needed to appropriately work with people that way. I was credentialed as a therapist, but I wasn't calling myself that. I fought hard to market myself, to network, and build my practice. I got a few clients here and there and worked part-time. It was nerve-wracking. I wanted the health coaching so badly and the payout from it, but it wasn't happening. My expenses were high because of overhead from the office.

I put up so much resistance to being a mental health professional. I had the credentials and the insurance paneling; I just didn't want to be that. It felt similar to being in active addiction and not wanting to accept that I was an alcoholic. Obviously, having a private therapy practice was a positive step, but it felt like an awkward fit. I built up a wall with negative beliefs about myself and my abilities. I was focused on being a health coach, which was clearly not working out. I know the loving hand of God was right there in this dilemma, guiding me through the muddy water of discernment toward being who I really was, and building my practice. It finally took my husband saying to me, "Why don't you just embrace being a therapist?" Yet I still resisted, before surrendering to the truth. Ryan was right. I asked myself again and again why was I turning my nose up at this. What was that about? Was it lack of skill, confidence, imposter syndrome, or maybe shame? Fear of showing up in that way, being vulnerable. What if I failed? What if clients didn't like me? Or I marketed myself as a therapist, people came, and I didn't serve them well. My husband believed in me. The insurance companies who accepted me onto their panels felt I was qualified. I needed to learn to believe in myself. To embrace the gifts I had been blessed with and use them for good. Sometimes quickly, sometimes slowly.

The rent went up, I didn't have the clients to support my practice, and I was given an opportunity from a former employer that I couldn't refuse. The best of both worlds. Being part of a large group practice where clients were consistent while also gaining the space to build my own private practice. I met my friend and former boss at a local Starbucks. We were catching up like old friends. He was a cyclist; I was training for marathons, so we had a lot in common. He was also a husband, a dad, and a Christian. He asked me how things were going with the practice, and I shared openly about the good and the bad. I remember there was a small feeling of shame tainting the conversation as I recounted the money I had invested and the lack of return I had received. It was a sour taste in my mouth like biting into a lemon slice coated with sugar before that shot of tequila.

Then it was his turn. He described for me how his large group practice was set up, that he had all the billing and support staff there, as well as plenty of office space. What he needed from me was a few hours a week to see his group clients, then I could see my own clients in their office space free of charge. I remember taking it all in and doing a quick review of the opportunity being presented. I was looking for the loophole, the scam. It wasn't my natural way to assume that someone would be so compassionate and generous towards me. Surely, he wasn't offering me office space for free. It was the break I needed at just the right time. It was the loving hand of God yet again coming into my life at Starbucks and offering me a way. I got in the car and called Ryan and told him what happened. I listened to his happiness come through the other end. I still wasn't sure what was going on, and I didn't know why he was so happy. I said, "I think he just offered me free office space." Ryan confirmed that and again congratulated me. I asked, "Why would he do that?"

Ryan simply replied, "Because that's what people do."

I didn't truly understand that. I had gotten sober in AA surrounded by hundreds of people who showed up, shared their message of hope, held out their hand in greeting, expecting nothing in return. I saw women find help with childcare, housing, and transportation. I had someone help me while I was pursuing my social work licensure, for free. Yet this was so baffling to me. I guess I always lived as though people did things expecting something in return, and many do. Accepting the "gifts" of others was challenging for me. I brushed off compliments. It took me years of being on the receiving end of "help" to realize that yes, that is what people do. Being of service sends good vibes to the universe, cleanses the soul, and gives peace.

In my 30's, I was still hustling for that sense of belonging, for the people who would accept and love me. I knew deep in some corner of my existence that I was a good mother, but the struggles of managing strong personalities challenged this. The angst of uncertainty, judgement and fear were nagging away at my soul most of that decade. I felt other women were more at peace with themselves, especially sober women. What was the missing link? Why did fear have such a stronghold on my heart?

I remember when I celebrated my ten-year sober anniversary. I was attending my home group meeting regularly but not really doing much else. The kids were busy with their activities; Ryan was building a career.

That year had been rough. We had struggled with parenting challenges, made some difficult decisions on how to get help for those. We moved our kids from their school and were preparing to transition them. There was no peace or contentment on the inside for me. There was fear. I mostly feared the future, what would happen with the kids, how they would turn out. What if we weren't doing it right? I shared from the podium at AA meetings and divulged some of the struggles I had over that previous year. I was a bit gloom and doom. I was grateful to be sober and alive, as I never expected to live that long. I was also in a lot of pain. I remember sharing how annoyed I was that at ten years sober, I was still working on some of the things I viewed as early sobriety issues. Why wasn't I further along? Ten years seemed like an eternity; I felt I should be more evolved by then. But I wasn't. The feelings of defeat, heartache, and loss I was feeling at the time were real.

Standing there in front of a room of other alcoholics in 2012, many of whom I had known for ten years, I had a feeling of, "I am still not enough. I have this big life, these beautiful children, a hardworking, handsome loving husband who is a great dad." I had been sober for ten years; I was proud of that. I had no desire to drink, and I had a deep relationship with a higher power. Life was still challenging. Parenting kids was exhausting. Marriage takes incredible effort. I still hadn't fully found my voice, the ability to speak up for my own needs and desires, and follow through. I was on the boat, but I wasn't the captain. I can see now this is just another layer of the onion. A growth period perfectly designed by God to show me where I was still lacking in emotional sobriety, in trusting Him and loving myself. Building my private practice helped in this area.

There came a time for me as a mom, after staying home for many years to raise my children, that I needed more. I felt like the line between who I was as a person at the core, what I stood for and believed in, and my roles as a wife and mom became blurred. I didn't even remember my original identity, if I ever even knew it to begin with. And to be fair I was pregnant six months after I got sober, nowhere nearly enough time to understand who I truly was as a person, sober woman, wife or mother. I loved being a mom. I cherished the time I had with my kids and we were blessed to be able to care for them at home for so long. I remember one time one of the kids was complaining that they had to get up early to go to before care at school (which is only thirty minutes more than their usual day) and I quickly reminded them how lucky they were not to have to go to daycare at 6 a.m. every day. I knew any work I took on would still be part-time and flexible as I would still be the responsible party for their care on a daily basis, so honestly not too much would change for them. It was an honor to be able to give them this time, and I loved these school-age years.

Somewhere around this time, I started working with a new sponsor. My original sponsor, Betsy, couldn't have been more perfect for me at the time. She was loving and solid in recovery. She taught me so much, walked me through the steps, and loved me through the parts of early recovery that were excruciating. And she carried a Longaberger basket purse. I called her every day, we went to meetings together, and she introduced me to other sober women. I sat on her bed as she was recovering from mastectomy surgery, went to her wedding; it was just what I needed. Betsy was kind. She loved me.

When I started working on my 4th step, where I had to list out all the things I had done wrong, people I harmed, and resentments I had, I was excited. I was ready to unload all my transgressions to relieve myself of the insufferable awareness that I was the worst of the worst of all people. I wanted to lay bare the secrets I had been holding in for years. I used the Big Book to do this step and wrote my list down. The inventory felt like a weight, a boulder tumbling down a huge mountain range. Not straight down though, bumping into trees and other boulders along the way making the journey longer. I remembered hearing other people sharing they had pages and pages of offenses, but my list was short. This made me question if I had done it right.

Betsy came to my house, we sat out on my porch in the sun and fresh air while I shared what I had written. The initial excitement I felt had waned and transformed into anxiety and fear. I suddenly was incredibly aware of my character defects, of just how odd I was as a person. Betsy sat with me in silence while I shared. She listened and validated my feelings. She shared some deeply personal stories from her own time of active addiction as an effort to normalize my experience. I appreciated her willingness to be open and honest. As much as I love therapy, sharing in this way isn't something you can get in therapy. In my opinion, only another person who has struggled with substance abuse to the point where they lost themselves, made decisions they wouldn't have if they had been sober, and have given up everything for the drink or drug, can share this kind of space with you. It is one of the most beautiful things about being in connection with other addicts, building a healing community around you filled with junkies and drunks. It's how and why it works.

I wasn't judged or scolded for my transgressions. I wasn't lectured about the choices I had made and the people I had hurt along the way. I wasn't told how selfish I was for the lying, the covering up, the manipulation. I wasn't looked down on or made to feel less than her or anyone else. I felt loved. I was loved. This was not the cordial and polite kind of love. This kind cuts deep like the Colorado River forming the Grand Canyon over thousands of years. She told me this wasn't who I was, it was just what happened to me. This was my addiction. She agreed that my list wasn't long but remarked that it was big. She explained that now my healing could begin. I couldn't have imagined a better experience. I am grateful to this day for the relationship we had, for the space she created and shared with me, and for the love she taught me I could receive. The love I eventually learned to give. This woman taught me about the program and more importantly the principles of twelve-step recovery. Betsy followed the guidelines that were presented to her, learned to stay sober one day at a time, developed a relationship with a higher power, and created deep, loving connections with people she would not have otherwise mixed with had it not been for the rooms of AA. Because her life had been deep in the darkness of addiction, she had lived through being in the pit, her trauma and pain were real, and alcohol had been her solution.

When I got sober there weren't (at least not to my knowledge) a whole lot of other ways to get sober besides AA. Doctors, pastors, therapists, and family members recommended it to loved ones who seemingly couldn't handle their lives without the use of mood-altering, life-escaping substances. It's what we had. I am thankful that I was told early on by wise women that AA wasn't the only way to get sober, it was just the way they knew. That stuck with me. The alternative was white knuckling it through on my own without the support of other sober people. I didn't see an alternative, and I didn't feel the need for one. I was scared. My life had come to a screeching intersection of good and evil. I had to make a decision to do something huge, make a change, or lose it all. I showed up, listened, and did what I was told.

Over time Betsy and I fell away. I don't know how this happens exactly; we just slowly started to lose touch. She had a son with some complicated special needs which took a lot of her time. I was busy with my kids and husband, and my relationship with Betsy faded. I believe we grow out of people sometimes. Ages and stages present us with new needs, and eventually that's what happened with Betsy and me. There wasn't a problem or incident—no hard feelings. I stayed sober, and I assume she did too. I didn't have a sponsor for a while. I was just cruising through life. It wasn't recommended to do the program alone, and not in the beginning. Connection is the opposite of addiction.

I was in need of some big change, a swift kick in the butt really. I needed the loving hand of a well-studied AA student to guide me through the next level of recovery. My marriage, although good, was challenging. We had some more learning to do about relating to each other. The onion gets peeled, and sometimes more pain is revealed. I had more work to do on my own personal growth. I had to listen to that still, small voice deep inside. There was learning left to do on my own needs and desires, roles as partners, and as parents. In order to build more emotional sobriety, even at over a decade sober, I needed to do more work. I prayed for God's will for me. I prayed for what I needed and was given a new sponsor. A tough, old school, AA woman with lots of sobriety, a husband, and kids. I needed someone with a similar lifestyle, someone who could relate to the stressors I was facing. I didn't know I needed someone that was tough as nails, but that's what I got. Her name was "Mary Anne." She helped me move my sobriety from just on par to AMAZING. Her tough outer layer was intimidating, scary even, but her heart was good. She would listen but never enable. Mary Anne put up with my whining and complaining and constant overwhelm. She taught me valuable lessons.

One lesson was to stop repeating my list of tasks and commitments over and over and over again. I remember sitting in the gym parking lot crying the blues about everything I had to do, I felt completely overwhelmed by it all. Mary Anne stopped me and said, "Stop repeating your to-do list. By now you have probably done that several times already today. You have told me, you've told your husband, you've probably called your mom, called who knows who else, and you have retold this same list repeatedly. No wonder you feel overwhelmed. Stop doing that. Look at your day or your list and then ask yourself, "What one task do I need to do right now?" and then do that. After that, just do the next thing." Simple, yet so powerful. I realized in that moment, that I was doing that same thing all the time. I created my own overwhelm and anxiety. The solution was as simple as needing to stop repeating my to-do lists repeatedly. She said, "Right now, you need to go home, put your groceries away, then go pick up your kids." This advice has stuck with me for years, and I continually share it with other sober women. We must break things down into smaller bite-sized pieces in order to get through this life, sober or not.

Mary Anne and I developed a friendship, our kids had common interests, and I genuinely loved her. She knew all the things about both of my lives, the one before 2002 and the sober one after. I felt safe with her, like I could deal with anything in my life. Her tough outer shell was likely for her own protection, one that kept others at a distance. I knew that was the case and I craved more; I wanted nothing more than a best friend. I don't think the feeling was mutual. She helped me, and no doubt she guided me through the process of building emotional sobriety. Yet that barrier was always there. I knew it, and I think that made me work harder at crossing it. I wanted intimacy so badly. I deeply desired connection with other women who understood me. Maybe I had unreasonable demands. Maybe I was just too much for her. Maybe she just didn't really like me anyway but was doing her AA duty to be my sponsor. I will likely never know.

The discomforts of life were still glaringly difficult for me. I was always so uncertain. I had no idea how to deal with that and I was turning to Mary Anne for the answers to everything that was my life. I didn't have the confidence yet to trust myself and my decisions, I wanted someone else to do it. I wanted someone to save me. I didn't intuitively know how to handle things. That is why Mary Anne played such a pivotal role in my recovery. I had to change. Despite the fact that Ryan and I had been together over twenty years I still couldn't fully be myself. I wasn't able to share my needs and desires or speak up for myself when things didn't feel right. Mary Ann showed me how to do this but more importantly she taught me that as an adult woman the only one that can truly help me is my God and myself. When she told me that, it hit a part of fear that hadn't been activated before. I looked at her and said "How do you do that".

Mary Anne pointed out how I had been allowing other people's voices to be the loudest in my life. Between Ryan, my parents, other professionals, friends, etc., I was giving them the power to direct my steps in a way that had become normal to me. The outside influences were strong, and I relied on them far too much. When this is your normal it is challenging to see where those voices might be manipulative and slightly controlling. This isn't always a negative thing, often we rely on important people in our lives to guide us. We aren't good at all things. Other people in our lives have skill sets that are different than ours. But for me it was the lack of confidence, the fear of emotional consequences, and the inability to be completely vulnerable with my closest people that prevented me from speaking up when I didn't like something or asking for something I needed. The dysfunction came from codependency and lack of trust in myself to make good decisions or be successful at anything.

We would meet to do step work and she taught me about creating healthy boundaries. This is a concept so many sober women struggle with because of negative thinking patterns that are alive and well in their minds. Very often they don't believe they are "allowed" to say no, or to make adjustments to schedules based on their own mental health needs. Learning what healthy boundaries are and how to create them was a pivotal start to me making huge changes in this phase of my recovery. I was grateful for her patience and care towards me as time after time I called in tears over the latest drama. She repeated the same phrases she taught me and encouraged me to look to God first to comfort myself and then do the next right thing. I could feel that slowly but surely, I was moving away from the scared little girl and into the power that God had instilled in me from the beginning.

My life was completely different from the decade before; I wasn't the same woman at all. The work is never over, though. The layers never stop peeling. For me more is always revealed. My insight changed, my willingness became real, and the wisdom I gained from life lessons allowed for more change. With the help of Mary Ann, I learned that I was worthy of my own desires, my own opinions, that it was okay if I shared them with my husband. That I should allow myself to be vulnerable enough to share them. This is what creates emotional intimacy in marriage and Ryan was desperate for me to do more of that.

For years I was afraid Ryan would be mad at me. Until one day my therapist said, "So what? He's allowed to be mad." At the time that terrified me but also was a huge eye opener. Anger is just a feeling, and everyone is allowed to have feelings. It doesn't mean he will divorce me. It doesn't mean he doesn't love me. It just means he's mad. This was hard for me. I began to establish myself more as an equal. Inequality wasn't something Ryan did, it was something I felt, because that quiet voice which spoke the negative belief "I'm not good enough", wasn't all the way healed. There were parts of me that didn't feel worthy for whatever reason. Then top it off with parenting three young children, sometimes feeling like a failure at that, considering my own next steps for building a career, not having deep connections with other women or God, and you have a whirling dervish! I was taught to embrace my own worth by practicing gratitude and respecting the ways I was in service to my family and the value of being a present, sober, and emotionally mature mother and wife. I had to recognize myself as valuable, loveable, and smart. That I had something to offer my marriage and family. I also had to understand and accept that I could take care of myself. In fact, it was literally my responsibility to be my own caretaker. The sad fact of adulthood is that we are all responsible, with the help of God, for taking care of ourselves. No husband, children, job, money, nor fitness level can meet all our needs. In the end, we are responsible for doing that. Of course, that doesn't mean we do it alone; it does mean that we could if we had to. This was an incredible shift for me and a direct result of my relationship with my second sponsor. She taught me that I was capable of taking care of myself and my kids by myself. That was literally my calling. For a while, I thought she meant that we didn't love our husbands, or we should leave them, or some other bizarre interpretation of what she was saying. What I came to realize was that I wasn't dependent on my husband. For most of my life I believed that Ryan was my lifeline (I still do in a way but it's much healthier now), that I literally couldn't live without him. Because I don't think I would have survived without him. I was very sick. I made bad choices consistently, dangerous choices in active addiction. But Ryan was always there, he was the stable force in my life. He was who I thought of before crossing certain lines. He was the love I always sought in my life even when we were "broken up." He was my life force. I believed at my very core I couldn't and wouldn't make it without him.

What I learned was that wasn't true. The truth was I wanted him. I wanted him badly because our love was real and deep and consistent and trustworthy. We had kids together and a home and a beautiful life. I didn't need him. I can remember the exact moment when this all came to the surface, and I spoke those very words outside of my mouth, standing in the galley kitchen of our home getting ready to go to a wedding. For our whole life I felt incredibly dependent on him. It wasn't at the conscious level at all. But deep on the inside, I was that scared little girl, latching on to the best thing she could to get her through life safely. And that was Ryan. The safe choice. The one who stuck by me, the one God sent to me to be the life raft and even when life tried hard to separate us, we never drifted apart. There were times throughout when I wanted to love him less; I tried. I wanted to be able to say I don't care and just leave. I would imagine he has felt the same. But the attraction was strong, the pull ever present. With all the efforts we made, we couldn't do it. I am grateful for that love. I am grateful for the commitment we both have to each other. For sitting in the therapist's office when we both professed to each other that no matter what we were deeply committed to each other. That seems rare in our society, and with all the things we have been through, the words and feelings we have slung at each other, the only explanation I have is God has been at work the whole time. And I am grateful.

The moment I spoke the words and truly meant it, "I don't need you; I want you", there was a major shift. It was like the work I had started doing in this second half of recovery was taking hold, guiding me in a new direction, unchartered territory for sure. I shocked myself with that. I truly hadn't talked back to Ryan much in our relationship at all. I held things in. I submitted to his wishes mostly. Not in a weird fundamental, we-only-wear-skirts kind of way. More like I love you, you know best, I don't even know how to express myself or what my real needs are kind of way. And Ryan is smart, wise beyond his years. He was like a fifty-year-old man at twenty. He is a planner, likes certainty and predictability. And also, a big feeler, which often shows up in slightly uncomfortable ways for those around him but because I know him, I know what's going on. Getting to the other side of discomfort and pain often means wreckage. And in this very moment I stood firmly on my feet with a confidence I had never experienced before and spoke those words out loud, and I meant it. I didn't want our marriage to end, much the opposite. I didn't want to leave or him to leave, but it was important that I believed that I could. It would be hard, undesirable, probably unbearable at times and of course everyone is affected in the most emotional ways. But

I believed I was capable. It was a jumping off place, one that separated that scared inner child from the strong, sober adult woman, mother, and wife that I was. Another spiritual awakening, which allowed me to continue building the self-worth and confidence I never had. All of this was a direct result of the complete package I had built for myself in my recovery.

There is never just one thing, one person, one nutritional change, one complimentary therapy. There are big things like the guidance from Mary Anne, the program of Alcoholics Anonymous, the healing I did with my therapist, and the ever-present loving support of my God. Then there are the tiny things that compound over time to create huge change. Establishing a strong morning routine, practicing positive self-talk, changing things in my physical health, asking for help, prayer, and drinking more water. So the work continues. Marriage and family life are both beautiful and brutal. Glennon Doyle coined the term "Brutiful" back in her Momastery blog days, and I latched onto that because it is completely relatable. It is likely the biggest challenge of life and also the most fulfilling experience, except it's hard to see that much of the time. And of course, not all relationships are healthy or safe. I would never advocate for anyone to continue to stay with a partner where there is abuse or severely toxic behavior toward her or the children. Those types need special care and support in order to make the best choice for everyone's protection. But relationships that are relatively healthy also need continuous attention, like cooking risotto. You can't stop stirring or it will stick to the bottom and burn. It takes consistent loving care. Compromise on so many levels and intense communication to keep things running relatively smoothly. And of course, commitment. We professed that commitment on more than one occasion sitting on a basement office sofa across from a therapist. Yet there was still a great deal of pain for each of us, things that were said and done that can never be undone, where the only thing left to do is forgive. Learning to communicate on a deeper level is worth the work. Also listening and validating the other person's feelings and being willing to sit with them through all the discomforts of life, without blaming and shaming. Harder than it sounds. And in my experience, it never ends.

You don't arrive at a marriage finish line, hands in the air, shouting, "We did it! We won the marriage race; it's over." I mean maybe at the end of life we can, but while we are in it, marriage takes grit. Building a marriage and raising children who become productive members of society is not for the faint of heart. But the joy is possible! I could feel a shift happening around that time. I was in a big growth spurt both emotionally and spiritually. I loved my family more than anyone can love anything, and I was deeply loyal and protective of them. But you can love your family and also love yourself. You can be confident in yourself and your abilities while also raising a family. There was this sense that no matter what I can be okay—the true definition of joy. And with any change in a system, especially a family, sometimes there is resistance. Often in relationships, one person is doing a lot of work or going through a challenging time and the other has more of a support role. Then those roles are switched with time. And the growth and change experienced by one partner can be uncomfortable for the other person, maybe even threatening.

A woman could feel deeply disappointed, left behind, and insecure if her husband suddenly begins making his health a priority, hanging out at the gym, and in healthy living Facebook groups. A man might be challenged if his wife does the healing work on her past, begins to love herself, and tap into the fierce nature that's been hanging out below the surface all the years he has known her. He might worry she will leave him and start a new life with all this confidence she has gained. Systems are affected by any change that occurs, so it's important to be sensitive and patient while going through the process. And the longer your family is together, most likely the more changes will occur because we are all always under construction. Dealing with life on life's terms, trying not to get pulled down by the quicksand of parenting, working, and marriage.

There are so many stories or moments I could point to that demonstrate these intense changes that occurred throughout my sobriety. And it's okay if your story or life doesn't line up just right with mine. Maybe you don't have kids, or you've never been married. Maybe you are in a same-sex relationship, you adopted your children, or you are divorced. It's no matter what the structure of your life is, what hits home for each of us is when we can relate to the feelings that another person shares regarding their life and the events of it. The way we handle the anxiety, stress, fear, and grief that come up on a daily basis while also staying sober. Most likely you can relate to the desperation I had during my sober bottoms (those times when it felt similar to the end of your drinking, but you were stone cold sober). The fear I have dealt with on so any levels, grief that is not just when someone passes, but the disappointment when people we love hurt us, often over and over again. None of us is the same. Our past lives aren't the same, our upbringing, our relationships, careers, or personal interests. That's what makes the world go round. But I am willing to guarantee if you are a woman who has been addicted to substances in the past, realized they were a problem in your life, got sober, and healed yourself, then you can relate.

What I have learned is that blessings from God, gifts freely given to me, might have been there before I got sober, but I couldn't see them. I couldn't know how precious they were, and I certainly couldn't enjoy them. There was no space for that, no peace. I was consumed all the time with the self-centered nature of my disease. Blinded to any blessings in my life, I was stuck in a self-pitying role that would have gone with me to the grave. If I had not made the decision to turn all of that over, to release the control that substances had over me, and go a different way, I would have missed it. In sobriety, I get to do all the things, The ugly, unglamorous things like cleaning or picking up dog poop, and the magical, spiritual things like listening to my daughter, kissing my dog, or being vulnerable with my husband. This is the stuff of life my friends, the things you may have never ever experienced before because you were in the grips of a raging addiction that robs you of everything good in your life. My life was not like that anymore and never had to be again if I continued doing the things I have been taught.

During the fall of that year, I was making my husband's annual photo calendar and I was really struck, maybe for the first time, by all the blessings and memories of the year. I felt astounded by all the things we experienced that year. Our life was full. I had been living alcohol free for over a decade and it was far from boring. I have had three children, stayed married, and was expanding my business. My heart and body became overwhelmed with gratitude and the tears began to flow. These were the blessings of sobriety.

When I first got sober, I had to change everything. That is what it takes to build a new sober life and be relatively happy in recovery. That change felt overwhelming, impossible. For me there was resistance every step of the way. Often, I did what was asked because I was too afraid not to. On the inside, I was having a full-blown tantrum. This got easier with time, until a bump in the road shook me up a bit. Those growth periods, as I call them, required a special kind of TLC. With extended sobriety when doing the work, I learned how to self soothe through these changes. Transforming daily habits and routines is a critical part of this process. Acts of self-love done in tiny baby steps over time. The old cliché being true that nothing changes if nothing changes.

For me, the best way to create sustainable impact in my life was to make small changes consistently over time. Living this way allowed my goals and dreams, no matter how far-fetched, to come into clearer view, and often eventual reality. My sober life was like eating a giant elephant, taking one bite at a time, digesting it, seeing what needs to be adjusted and continuing on.

I would never claim that my life in recovery has been easy, but I was taught and firmly believe, the process is simple. My own personality lent itself well to baby steps, growing one inch at a time. I can compare it to running a marathon. No one, even a highly experienced distance runner would say running a marathon is easy. And as someone who has done it, I can testify that it is super hard. This is so similar to trying to get sober. In active addiction, I couldn't even imagine not drinking. The lifestyle alone seemed boring, not to mention I had zero life skills to carry me on without the use of substances. When I landed in treatment I was overwhelmed with fear and anxiety at the magnitude of sobriety. There was no way I could stop drinking forever. My story wasn't even that bad. But just like training for a marathon, I learned to take the advice of those who had gone before me and moved through recovery in tiny baby steps. It wasn't easy and of course I wasn't going to have ten years' worth of wisdom and knowledge right away, but if staying sober and living a life in recovery was a goal for me, I could do it one day at a time. I could break down the program, the steps, the emotional growth into small segments and do what I could in that moment to live well and not drink. And then the next day, do the same thing. Then before I knew it, I put together weeks, months and years sober. The growth never ends. It felt impossible at the time, too big but I broke it into a million little things and my life got better.

Since getting sober I have used this concept to build the life I have today. I changed my own health (more than once) by looking at the outcome I desired and then made a plan to work towards that. I tapped into other interests and engaged in activities that supported them. I tried new things, like taking a hip hop class. I have learned the overwhelm I experience from a new thing or goal fueled by my passion, doesn't come from the desire. It is driven by my focus on the whole thing. The ending. And while I understand that some focus on desired outcome leads us in the right direction, the reason it can feel impossible is because we are focused on the whole thing. Marathon training and completion seemed extreme, but when I broke it down and decided to go out and buy some new sneakers and a cute outfit it was a simple task. A necessary step that moved me closer to the long-range goal. Like not taking a drink today feels cliché, but when done every day you stay sober.

In the beginning, I had to learn how to follow directions. I was taught to start my day with gratitude, asking God to help me not take a drink that day and helping me to know what His will was for me. I did that every day. I was also taught to contact my sponsor every day. This was important for me in early sobriety. Creating discipline in my life took time. Many people who struggle with alcohol are undisciplined. It does not always appear that way, as they might be high achievers, successful. I lacked the consistency, self-respect, and self-love that it takes to stick with something. I needed to be taught the value of doing certain actions every single day and to follow the direction of another person. I felt like I knew who I was told I was, or who I should be. I knew who I had been raised to be. It was the case for me like so many, despite the need to know who I was. Yet for decades I didn't understand. I learned to put healthy habits and routines in my life every day to build that discipline and ultimately trust in myself. I learned I could count on myself. This self-discovery work was part of my emotional sobriety process and took some time. In fact, I'm not done. I don't want to ever be done.

In those early years, weeks, and months of sobriety, every day felt like a struggle. I was learning how to move through life and feel all the feelings without substances. All I did was follow the directions of my sponsor and other guides I chose to help me. With time I was able to put more healing tools into place to further my emotional recovery, heal my relationships and live more spiritually connected. These resources were amazing and became my go-to strategies for dealing with life beyond recovery. With time I began to stand tall on my own two feet. I learned to intuitively know how to handle situations that used to baffle me. I never did it alone, but the support levels change with time.

Loss from death is painful; other losses we experience in life can feel just as intense. The experiences of loss have lingering effects on our emotions and ability to engage in healthy relationships. The loss of friendships, jobs, or even moving from one stage of life to another can seem worse than death. Living sober through so much loss can find you searching for other forms of relief. This is one reason why having a variety of support people is critical for well-being. If we have all our eggs in one basket, whether it is a spouse, a parent, or friend, if something goes wrong with that one person, you could be left utterly alone. Fellowship is not just for twelve-steppers. We need a variety of relationships we can count on, preferably some who also understand recovery to lean on in times of need. Cultivating this community is a priority in emotional sobriety, because when we look to those who have gone before us or the women who seem to be killing it in recovery, one quality they have in common is a strong network of women walking alongside them. People who get them. The pain that comes from the loss of friendship is deep and difficult to understand. I never think of friends and pain in the same sentence. I had lost a couple of friends to them moving to other states. That was hard because they were women I deeply loved. It is challenging to keep up with people after they move far away, especially when you are raising kids and working.

My second sponsor, Mary Anne, a woman I loved

and admired, cut me off after a falling out; I still don't understand why. She was strong, wise, and someone I counted on, maybe too much, to help me navigate the journey of my marriage and parenting. Until that point, I had never experienced the level of malice, almost hate, I felt from her. It was a deep and lasting discomfort that I felt for a long time. I am quite certain I didn't understand my own part in this situation. I have no clue why our relationship ended the way it did. There were words she said about me that were hurtful to the core, misunderstandings that involved not only me but also my children. I am certain I will never understand what really happened. I accept that, but it took a while to get there. I'm sure she was hurt too. Otherwise, why would she have acted that way? I put a great deal of effort and solicited help from Ryan, in formulating well thought out, heartfelt responses to her accusations and feelings. I apologized for my part in the situation on several occasions, but emotions ran hot. There was a fire in her that nothing I said or did was going to extinguish. Now I know that's not my job. I gave it my all, though. I put my whole heart into trying to reconcile, to being open minded to where I needed to grow. Sadly, her choice wasn't to stay in the difficult conversation but rather to cut me off completely, block me in every way she could from any contact with her.

The loss of Mary Anne as my friend and my sponsor was devastating for me. My ego was bruised. I wondered how someone who was supposedly close to me, knew intimate details about my life and recovery could abandon me? But much more was the loss of intimacy. The loss of friendship, that I thought was true and deep. Hindsight is always 20/20.

Now I can see part of this that belongs to me, but also much of it that doesn't. I did my part to make amends and work towards repair, and it wasn't enough. She didn't want that. I allowed myself the space I needed to grieve the friendship. To recall the details, notice where I could have done better but also acknowledge what I did well. To let go of the idea that she would be part of my life for the long haul. This was a process. I had times when I thought, "Why bother getting close to anyone? It's not worth it." But in all relationships, there is risk of being hurt. That's the nature of human existence. The connections we build are far more important than the risk of loss.

I learned that while community with others is integral, in the end only God and myself were responsible for taking care of me. I could not put that responsibility on a sponsor, on my husband, or on a friend. That lesson is one I am thankful to have learned, as I gained autonomy, boundaries, and the ability to speak my own needs.

CHAPTER 11

NOTHING WORTH DOING IS EASY.

Even with all I have experienced in my recovery, nothing was more personally challenging than the past five years. I could only assume that God had been preparing me along the way for what was to come. Strengthening my resiliency muscles and building the emotional sobriety one change at a time was the armor I needed. As our oldest daughter Grace made her way through middle school, we were faced with the decision of changing schools again. Should she continue at New Covenant or move on to a bigger private school? She wanted to move on. We scheduled a day at the bigger school, where she would shadow an enrolled student. She loved John Carroll High School. What's not to love? They had the bigger building, every academic and athletic opportunity one could ask for, and the social community like that on a college campus. She was drawn in immediately.

This was the most challenging disagreement Ryan and I ever had. I was being triggered in ways I couldn't identify at the time. We disagreed about what was best for our daughter, what would be safe for her, and where she would get the moral training to develop a close relationship with God moving into adulthood. New Covenant is a special place, one filled with love and discipline and academic rigor. It is not without its problems, as is true in any school. Kids act out there, just like everywhere else. The discipline problems at New Covenant are nowhere near the magnitude of those in bigger schools. And the difference in public versus private schools is also prevalent. Our experience with the private school was one of collaboration with family to work through issues when they arise. I love that part about it. The support we would have in training up our teenagers to become productive, good problem solvers, and capable of defending their world view in any environment. Ryan and I disagreed about it. Although the classical education offered at New Covenant was phenomenal and I would recommend it to anyone, the school was small. They had one class per grade with limited resources. They didn't offer many of advanced placement classes or competitive sports. They didn't have fancy computer and science labs, but they produced incredible graduates. Kids who went off to college were completely prepared for what was beyond high school. It certainly was difficult when shown both options to choose to stay there. The negatives of moving were mostly fear based. I knew that there were kids at every school who chose to stay on track, who avoided the party scene, who stayed focused on their goals, and didn't get in trouble. It came down to who their friends were; they all had choices.

Ryan was in favor of Grace changing to the new, bigger school. I wanted her to stay at New Covenant. We tried to work through it. Ryan really wanted me to be on board because he didn't want us to continue to be in disagreement. I was being strangled by the fear of my own past, and I wanted the exact opposite for my kids. I wanted them to choose an easier path, the one less traveled and without as much pain. I knew that there wasn't a compromise in choosing a high school for our child, we had to pick one. You can't go to half of a school. I also knew there was no way I was ever going to be comfortable with the change. I spent weeks and months and those feelings didn't go away for a very long time. I never wanted to drink, but I did want relief. I wanted the pain to go away. I wanted someone else to make these hard choices, and I wanted to protect my daughter from everything. Logically, I knew that wasn't possible. Anyone who has parented knows you can give your children all the things, your very best, and they will go into the world in the way they choose. I knew in the depths of my soul that I couldn't rubber stamp this choice with my approval, but I also wanted peace and harmony in my marriage. After deep contemplation, prayer and consult with trusted advisors, I came to the conclusion that I could let this go. I could turn this decision over to my child, support her with deep love and affection and let the chips fall where they may. The fear was still present, and I didn't believe it would ever go away. But there was also acceptance and a trust in my husband without regret. I shared with Ryan that I could not see myself ever agreeing with this decision, that I did not agree with his rationale for the change, but I did support him. And the only way for us to have peace in our marriage and move forward as a family was for me to let go. In the end, the decision was made to allow Grace to make her own choice. The shiny object won.

None of this happened in a vacuum. We had two other kids, our jobs, and our marriage. Around this time our second daughter, Nora, started to struggle with heightened anxiety, very common for middle school girls. Nora was a high achiever, a perfectionist with a great head on her shoulders and a genuinely good heart. She was fully engaged in riding horses since she was six years old. Years earlier she had quit her other sports so she could ride exclusively. And she was good. She loved her animals, worked hard with her trainer, and in caring for the horses. It's hard. It's messy, and it never ends. She got connected at age 11 with a local woman well known in the horse community as someone who brought on young farm hands to teach them. Nora worked at this woman's farm all summer, she traveled with the owners to shows, she was there when the vet and blacksmith came, and she was present for and participated in several labor and delivery processes for the woman's horses. Nora has had more experience with horses in her young life than most people will ever see. It was her passion. This experience proved to be both a blessing and a curse for Nora, all the while we touted it as work ethic, responsibility, mentorship. As parents, Ryan and I love with the biggest love I have ever known, the attachment is real. But we don't know what we don't know. We couldn't know.

Her anxiety was manageable for the most part, and she had a great therapist. We know that hormones contribute to mood regulation and that the onset of adolescence can certainly bring on feelings of anxiety and depression. She started learning coping skills and how to regulate the feelings that were contributing to her current fears. Nora began having stomach issues. She said her stomach hurt all the time. We thought it was from food. We recommended diet changes for her. We thought it was stress, so we used essential oils, therapy, journaling, etc. She was in pain. Seeing my child in pain also hurt me. I was told somewhere along the way that we are only as well as our most hurting child. I truly understood what that meant. The anxiety started showing up more around cleanliness and health; she was a bit of a germaphobe. And then someone at school got sick and that sent Nora into a tailspin. It was a challenging and emotional time.

The struggle and the pain she experienced were at times unbearable. I didn't know what to do, and the struggle to do the right thing was constantly on my mind. For a week or so it was a challenge to get Nora out of bed and to school. She refused to go to school. She would get visibly upset and lash out when we tried to wake her up for school, which created a lot of emotions for everyone in the house. We had to physically remove her from bed and help her get to the bathroom and get to school. While there, she was distraught and texting me to let her come home. The biggest blessing during that time was our school. They were able to collaborate with us to build an environment for her that was supportive and loving. They created a safe space for Nora in the principal's office where she was allowed to go and just sit if she needed to. There were two senior girls there that my daughters had befriended, and one was very close with Nora. We involved one of the senior girls in the process as a person she could connect with during the school day when things got tough. I am forever grateful to New Covenant, the staff, and students there who supported our family. I can't imagine navigating all of this without a team of people around us.

Parenting really does take a village to use the famous cliché. And parenting sober takes fellowship and a strong relationship with an energy source outside yourself. I don't know what I would do without God to rely on for fatherly love, for guidance and mercy.

I share stories about my children, as respectfully as possible, not to be embarrassing or bring attention to myself but quite the opposite. This is to help any other mother out there who thinks they are alone. I share my perspective and feelings on the situation, how I worked through them or survived, and how I stayed sober and relatively well. I also do this after having worked through the feelings myself and with the blessing of each of them.

We reached the height of Nora's anxiety with our vacation to trip to Sedona, Arizona, the Grand Canyon, and Zion National Park. It was the first time to those locations for all of us except Ryan. I was so excited; the adventure of traveling brings a thrill. Grace and Derek were relatively excited, as much as any pre-teens get revved up about a trip with family and a week away from friends. But Nora was adamantly opposed to the trip. We talked about it, but we weren't able to identify what it really was about traveling that upset her. Maybe she didn't know. She wasn't afraid of flying, all she said was she didn't want to go. I know she worked on it with her therapist in the weeks leading up to us leaving. Still, she consistently said, "I'm not going on that trip." In our home we were very positive, we used breath work, had essential oils, and we talked, creating a lot of space for her to express herself and for us to support each of our children however we could.

The night before our trip, I remember sitting with her and praying, soothing her as best I could. She seemed nervous. Nothing in my life prepared me for what happened the next morning. I knew she was going to have a hard time and after going through physically removing her from her bed sometimes for school, working hard just to get her in the building. We had to get up before 4:00 a.m. to leave for the airport. Everything was packed the night before; Ryan and I got the kids up and prepared to leave. We gently worked with Nora through that waking up process. She said, "I'm not going." I remember praying that morning that God would just come into our home, that He would work with Ryan and me, so that we would not do or say anything that would cause more harm than help, but mostly that He would comfort Nora. I asked that He would wrap His arms around her and give her what she needed. The struggle ended with Ryan, Grace and Derek waiting in the car for us, ready to go. I had to physically remove Nora from her bed and put my pre-teenage daughter into our Yukon. I did all of this while listening to her cry and flail. I felt like the worst person in the world. What had I done? I got in the car, and Nora and I cried the entire drive to the airport. I wondered what our other kids were thinking. I felt sad for them, that they had to experience that, but also grateful they did. Life isn't all sunshine and roses. In our family, we stand up and we come alongside those who are hurting. But it didn't exactly look like that on this day. I felt depleted, empty, completely exhausted. Were we doing the right thing? How was this trip going to go? Where do we go from here? So many questions and unknown answers to what appeared to be a raging internal crisis for my child. Nothing in life before had prepared me for this level of confusion and pain. I am damn glad I had been sober for a while. I had a program of recovery in my life that helped me stay sane. I knew that no matter what was going on around me, I was going to make it. I was strong on the inside. God came into our car and helped soothe her, soothe all of us. By the time we got to the airport, parked and walked to our gate, she was calm.

We ended up having a really nice trip. Nora talked a little about her fear of the trip but still no real finger on what caused so much anxiety about it. She was confident she would be fine on the way home.

I had several spiritual experiences on this trip looking around at the incredible beauty that God has created right here in our own country. A land I had never seen before in all my four decades of life. Climbing to the top of huge rock structures, and looking around at the incredible earth is spiritual. Viewing the Colorado River, the very thing that cut through the land to form these canyons, through Angel's Window was an out-of-body experience for me. Breathtaking and frankly unbelievable. I have a photo of that view in my office and when I see it, I remember the possibilities of life, the power of the earth, the forces pressing down on our land, the change that happens slowly over time. In my most vulnerable moments, I remember my Nora, her young innocent face filled with fear, and what that time must have been like for her. If I could have taken away her pain in that moment, God knows I would have. I have learned that the bravest thing I can do as a mom is not to protect my kids from pain, but rather to hold their hand and walk with them in the midst of it.

When we got back, she processed a lot with her therapist about the trip. I don't know all the details, but one thing Nora shared with me was that her therapist

and painful, like someone was slowly twisting a cork-
screw into my heart one turn at a time.

During this period, I was using the tools I had ac-
quired throughout my recovery. I was praying, reaching
out to other women, exercising, eating healthfully, and
staying sober. I still had no idea what was going on with
my own child. This was a powerlessness I had never felt
before. Until one day, I can only assume through the intervention of God, I decided to let it go. I let go of the
idea that I had anything to do with any of this; I also
let go of the idea that I could control or change it. God
revealed to me that none of this was my fault at all. I
hadn't done anything wrong. Quite the opposite, Ryan
and I had done most things right. We had provided a
loving home and family for all of Grace's fifteen years.
We raised her with basic rules and expectations to keep
her safe, a moral code, and more love than the projec-
tive heart from the Love-A-Lot Carebear. This was not
my fault. I wasn't saying that I wouldn't be willing to
humble myself before her and admit when I was wrong,
because I would. I realized that whatever was going
on with her was her own attempt at having control,
of building independence, and pulling away. I decided
to let Grace go. Not turn my back on her. Never! But
to let go of the illusion that I had any control over her,
her thoughts, or her decisions. Let go of the idea that
I could change anyone or make them do anything. Just
let it all go. In Al-Anon they call this "detach with love."
I can love you from a distance. In this case the situation
came to an end in a few weeks' time, and she was back to

speaking with me. Our relationship challenges continued for several years, though. I was more at peace after
making the decision to let her go. I was able to sleep at
night knowing that my side of the street was clean. I
hadn't done any known harm and saw that God was at
work. I truly believe that God gives us our children to
be their guide. They don't belong to us; they never did.
They are their own individuals from the moment they
are formed. They need a lot of care and attention and
training up, but they aren't ours. It feels like they are
because we grew them in our bodies, and it seems like
we almost have rights over them. The reality is that we
were just a holding cell for these beautiful creatures. We
are given the opportunity to help them come into this
world and let them do their own thing. Our job is only
to walk alongside them, teach and guide them through
life, and try our darndest to keep them safe and alive.
When they became teens, the realization that they are
in control of their choices, was painful and also beautiful. Grace was simply beginning her stage of building
a life separate from her parents, figuring out her place
in her world.

One struggle in parenting is finding the balance
between creating autonomy, having expectations and
rules, and allowing children to have fun. The challenge
in parenting sober is doing all of that, with the atti-
tudes, heartbreaking choices, and consequences, without the use of mood-altering substances. I spent many
nights wondering how other moms did it. Many of
them drink! In my view, none of us should be "using"

substances of any kind to relieve our stress from parenting or work or grief. Alcohol is poison. It is literally ethyl alcohol, a poison, that we add coloring and ingredients to in order to make it palatable. It has no nutritional value and is completely detrimental and unnecessary for human consumption. But I would be lying if I said that I didn't think about it often as just the relief I could use to get through this particular stage of life. In recovery, we are called to be better than that, to use the toolbox of resources we are taught along the way to relieve our stress, maintain our health, have fantastic sex, and climb the ladder at work. Putting on the armor of emotional sobriety takes effort, time, and intentionality. Every single day. When does it get easier? I am no expert but maybe not until we are in heaven.

We struggled to have clarity on what was going on socially, as we didn't know any of her new friends or their parents. Grace became close with a girl right away, so I began communicating with that girl's mother. The two of us developed a sort of partnership and were on the same page with rules and boundaries. There were things going on with both girls that neither of us had any clue about. Grace was extremely private and secretive about her life. Her grades were below average that year, and she was cut from the junior varsity volleyball team. She was grounded on more than one occasion, and she was running with a "fast" crowd. We were learning during this time, too. We were learning her. Who was this young woman? What did she want for her life? How could we support her?

She had a great therapist. I believe all kids should be connected with a therapist by the time they are in middle school. It's a tough time no matter who you are, and they need the support of other adults to help them navigate through it. It was a challenging time.

Nora was struggling at New Covenant as an eighth grader and every day complained about being there. Derek was doing well in fifth grade. They were all busy with sports, friends, and other school activities. Our best friends moved to Florida, and I was building a private practice and a home office. I was spiraling down into some older patterns; not fully, but just a gentle slide. I was searching for something, anything to give me some clarity on my own purpose, my desires, and my goals. With Grace getting older, one clearly distancing herself and boldly expressing her independence, the next one right on her heels, it's easy to feel unneeded. I was sad a lot, confused by the sadness, and I was filled with fear. I felt pretty certain things were not going to go well for Grace based on her behavior and choices thus far.

In the midst of raising adolescents, I was building my practice again. There was a longing inside of me to serve more. To reach more women across the world, to show them all the things I had discovered in recovery. I had zero clue what that meant or what it would entail, but there was a fire inside. I started listening to podcasts, reading blogs, reading books; whatever content I could get my hands or ears on, I consumed it. I don't have a business degree, a marketing background, or any real understanding of how to read a P&L sheet, but I do have A LOT of passion for people. I also have a few years of sober time, a clinical background, training in natural wellness, and my own experiences that have informed my work to build a life I don't need to escape from. Thank God Ryan is a great business manager, accountant, and advisor. He is the brains of the business, and I get to help people. I have never been one for the easy way and the calling was as loud as a rooster at 5:00 a.m. Pursuing this dream of helping sober women to build confidence beyond recovery, renewed my spirit, and gave me purpose. When I set my mind to something, I am all in. Head-first. Blood, sweat, and tears.

I knew that nothing worth doing is easy. The fear of failure, imposter syndrome, and burnout were obstacles on more than one occasion, and I have cried about it. I remember being in a professional workshop with a brilliant marketing expert learning how to build an online course and market it. I had been absorbing all the information, learning about platforms, email marketing, and Facebook groups. I was not afraid of hard work. I usually dove headfirst into whatever the challenge was and went for it.

We had one of our group coaching calls and were working through some of my marketing materials. In the midst of that, I just fell to pieces on the screen in front of everyone. Raw and exposed, full of fear and uncertainty, knowing the whole time I had to do this, I couldn't give up. The ups and downs were ever-present. Usually, I recognized it when it was happening. I had great mentors in my life and a toolbox full of resources to draw from.

Serving sober women was a calling that came from God, and a path that was carved out for me from the beginning. I didn't know it at the time. I tried to avoid it. Just like I tried to resist embracing the fact that I was a clinician and should be a therapist rather than a health coach. When I began building my business, I stayed in the anxiety niche because it felt safer. Most people were pretty comfortable talking about anxiety, and I didn't have to cross any personal boundaries. That was fine, I was building an audience and materials that were necessary for them. The missing element in the whole thing was authenticity. Until I was able to completely embrace who I am and what I am, I knew I wouldn't fully arrive in my life. I had to be my true authentic self. I had to share it all. That level of vulnerability doesn't come naturally to me. I don't like it. I don't want to expose myself like an open wound just waiting for the salt to be poured on. However, when I do the rewards so much greater than any potential consequences. The true stories started to be told, at first slowly and then like the biggest purge.

In 2019, our family started down a muddy avalanche that brought with it change, pain, and some of the biggest blessings we had ever known. In May of that year, the company where Ryan worked for almost nineteen years began the process of being sold. After giving it his all trying to lead them into the future, Ryan was instead the first cost-cutting casualty to dress up the financials for the sale. While there was a financial pay-out that came with it, our family lost a generous salary that afforded us the opportunity to provide a life for our children filled with opportunities. We had three kids in private school at the time, I was working part-time (for the income) and building my business. We had a lovely home, two cars, a gym membership, and a beautiful dog. Our family was healthy and relatively happy despite the teenage challenges we weathered. I was a strong, confident, sober woman. This news was the kind that shocks you to the core and brings a whole new level of fear. It was a humbling experience to sit in the kitchen and tell our three children this news. There was the obvious financial impact, however, I knew my husband was incredibly employable and qualified. He would be an asset to any company.

Beyond that was the emotional toll for him. Jobs are so much more than just jobs in many cases. They become an identity, even if we tried not to make them so. Ryan gave more hours a week than he should have, traveled, strategized, sacrificed, and loved that job and his colleagues. Unfortunately, his vision for the future didn't align with the owner's, and like that, it was over. The news hit like a death. He got busy making it his job to find a job. That is exactly what he did. I wanted to do my part, to fill the void somehow, but my mini-mal salary could barely cover our groceries. I was heart-broken for him. He had given so much for so long. I didn't understand why this had happened, but I knew that God had a plan for us. I had faith that Ryan would find something to provide for us because that's the kind of man he is. His emotional ups and downs were channeled into networking, working with a job coach, lunches and dinners with old colleagues, feet to the ground, get-it-done work. The questions from friends and family came non-stop. Of course, they were just interested, concerned even, but in my view, it was the only thing everyone could talk about. We went to bed and woke up thinking about his job and our finances. We prayed hard for God's will while we enjoyed Ryan being home more. As expected, he found a job in thirty days. The new position was not without its challenges, but it also had some perks like being in our local area. We all breathed a sigh of relief.

At that same time, Nora was preparing to go to high school with her sister, and Derek was entering sixth grade. Nora had been riding horses for many years, even purchased her own pony, and was training him to sell him for a profit to buy another horse. She worked hard with him, was there in the cold and rain, and dedicated her energy to making him the perfect pony. Her show season was difficult that summer. She also had decided to try out for the high school soccer team, which meant a lot of physical training to revive her soccer skills and get in shape. She was a natural athlete, but the time and the physical toll was demanding. Her interest in riding began to wane, and as we started the process of selling her animal, she decided she didn't want another one. We encouraged Nora and supported her through the process and, we knew she was changing.

Those same feelings I had experienced a year earlier with Grace came flooding in and I was overwhelmed with sadness, discontent, and confusion.

While I was excited for Nora to start her new school, so proud of her work ethic and ability to make a high school soccer team after not playing the sport for years, I was also sad. I knew this was part of the process of growing up, but the grief was obvious, raw, and real. In my mind, I was losing another child to young adulthood, to friends. Nora and I had spent a lot of time together with horses for many years. In my view it was our thing, a huge connection and opportunity for me to be with her, to learn more about her, to know her. In what seemed like the blink of an eye, that was gone. I respected her desire to do other activities. I was terrified that she would turn on me the way Grace had. The school year started off with healthy boundaries, providing loving and cautious support in their social lives, and riding the waves of two high schoolers and the gentle ease of our growing middle schooler. We were getting into our routine until we were blindsided by a seemingly insurmountable challenge in November.

Earlier that month I had a professional situation regarding my social work license that was extremely scary, disruptive, and emotional. My license was due to renew at the end of October and the continuing education credits I submitted were not accepted by the Board. This blow was massive as my license was not renewed and you cannot run a clinical practice without a license. I was shocked and completely caught off guard. I immediately went into problem-solving mode. I had no idea what was even happening as this was not something I had experienced before. The thought of having to shut down my practice made me nauseous. What would my clients do? What would they think of me? Every single day for a week I was on the phone with the board, doing additional continuing education, scrounging up any credits I had earned anywhere to get this thing done. At one point I was on the phone with my clinical supervisor, a woman who offers a group for EMDR therapists to grow and learn together, to see if any of our meetings counted as credits. I completely lost it on the phone with her. I have never experienced that hyperventilating type of crying before, but it took over. She was compassionate and kind and said she would do whatever she could to help me. I didn't even know what I needed other than some type of miracle. I kept contacting other colleagues, people I had worked for, and anyone I could think of that might have advice or resources. It was the longest, most draining week I had experienced in quite some time. Finally, I got the credits done and was back in business.

No sooner than my tears were dried, and clients were back in my office, did I receive a phone call from the high school on a Wednesday afternoon. They asked that I come pick up our daughter Grace; she was being suspended. The day before she and her friend were smoking marijuana in the school bathroom. Shock, rage, fear, and sadness were some of the emotions I experienced. I walked into the school with a knot in my stomach. As I was being escorted to the dean of discipline's office, Nora saw me. She was visibly upset and asked me what was going on. Seeing her sadness and fear was heart-wrenching. Both of my girls were hurting. Then I saw Grace. She looked small in the office chair, child-like even. We argued; I was mad and sad. The car ride home was quiet. We had five days until the review board would hear her case and decide whether she would be readmitted or expelled. Our family supported Grace in the most loving way, offering words of encouragement and sharing stories from their own sordid youth. My husband's Bible study group was praying for her. Ryan and I were upset. We were also angry. How could she do this, and what had she been thinking? We also knew the mistakes we had made. The following Tuesday was the day of the review board where they would hear her case and allow Grace to advocate for herself. Then we would wait for the decision regarding expulsion from the school. We worked with Grace on formulating her position and advised her to be honest and real. At the hearing, Grace spoke, then we shared our views on the situation, how our family was handling this at home, and our expectations of Grace moving forward. The phone call came from the principal later that night. She was expelled. My heart just broke for Grace and our family. Tough decisions about where she would go from that point were thrust upon us. Grace was obviously upset and didn't want to be comforted by any of us. I can only imagine what was going through her mind, how she felt when she told her friends, receiving messages from grandparents and extended family. We all understood it was her choices that landed her in that position and even though we can accept consequences we can still be really sad about them.

The holidays were just after this; they brought a refreshing change of pace. I was proud of my family for coming around Grace the way they did. I was extremely grateful. The school was an adjustment for Nora now too, as she got a lot of questions from her peers and no longer had her big sister there. Even Derek experienced some level of discomfort as word spread through town and other kids learned about what happened. Navigating our community, social circles, and sports fields knowing everyone had heard what happened with Grace was challenging. There were two women who reached out to me right after Grace was expelled. They were both friends with kids in Nora's grade. One sent a text that said "I am so sorry to hear the news about Grace, it could have been any one of us. We are thinking about you." Her message meant the world to me. I was actually shocked to receive her text, but I was grateful. I will be sure to do the same if I can ever comfort another parent in that situation. The other woman called because they had an older child at the same school who was graduating. Their child had the same thing happen, and she was offering her experience and advice. This level of outreach was special, unexpected, and greatly appreciated. One thing I know for sure is we never really know what is going on for people that we cannot see.

We handled the transfer to the public high school,

Grace swam on their swim team, and met some new friends. Outwardly she seemed to be handling the change well, but there was a lot of sadness, grief, and some depression brewing under the surface. We could tell she was struggling to express her feelings and we offered her the best resources we could. There were other teenage issues along the way that created drama, the need for discipline, drug testing, and therapy. Every time something happened, it felt like someone was just grinding their work boot into the back of my head. I was questioning myself, our parenting, our rules.

Then the pandemic hit. In March 2020, the schools shut down, my husband's company transitioned all employees to work from home, and every activity was canceled. We both still had jobs to support our life, and we were healthy. There was some real blessing to slowing down our lives. We spent more time together as a family, Derek built a fire pit out of materials we had around the house, we started learning more about birds and we played a lot of Yahtzee. Our mental health took a hit, though. It came in waves for each of us over the course of the year. Grace's depression got worse with online school. She slept a lot, had trouble waking up in the morning, and didn't attend her classes. She did get a job at McDonald's on March 1, 2020, which we viewed as a total Godsend for her. She was motivated to go to work. With time Grace began having suicidal thoughts that became overwhelming after quarantine started. Nora even came to us saying how concerned she was about Grace and all she talked about was her depression.

One Saturday afternoon we finally confronted her about what was really going on. Ryan and I asked the hard questions and sat with Grace while she cried. The confusion, anxiety, fear, sadness, and grief were gut wrenching. We made the decision to take her to an in-patient facility to be evaluated. We agreed to let the facility staff decide the course of action and plan for her treatment. The hour drive to the facility was brutal. I remained as calm as I could. She didn't talk much; I can't even imagine what she was feeling. She didn't want me to be upset. We parked the car, grabbed her bag, and headed for the door. As we walked in, Grace looked at me and said, "Do you think they can help me here?" I wanted to reassure her, I wanted to reassure myself.

I said, "Yes, I do."

Even though I had worked at social services, been involved in admitting young people, had practiced as a clinical therapist, and advised other families to do exactly what I was doing right now, I literally felt completely powerless. I had no idea what to expect. I felt alone and terrified. This was my child, my first baby. I had attended field trips with her, watched her dance recitals, soccer games, and swim meets. We took her to the American Girl Doll shop in New York City, taught her how to ski at Deep Creek Lake, ate banana taffy with her at the beach, and went with her to her first homecoming dance pre-party. I had zero preparation or emotional bandwidth for any of this. How was this happening, why was this happening? It was the hardest thing I have ever done. I wished for an escape.

My eyes were almost swollen shut by the time I got home that evening. The crying continued for the nine days she was gone. I know there are many mothers out there who have experienced this and now so many more because of the pandemic. It was unbearably hard on kids. There was a lot of pain in that time period, the kind that feels like something was literally ripped off of you, like a life-sized Band-Aid. So many questions, what if's, whys. I am grateful for a strong recovery in my life. I am thankful for a supportive family and a husband that was feeling it too but who also really stepped up at that time. There are so many blessings in this life. The details of her story and treatment are private and only hers to share. For me, although this was one of the deepest heartaches I have felt, it turned out to be just what Grace needed. After her stay, there was more work to be done, but things got much better. She got better, and that is all I could have ever hoped for.

The pandemic brought a lot of ups and downs, and a lot of feelings as we worked our way through it. The girls enrolled in distance learning to start the 2020-2021 school year, but Derek was at school in person. Ryan was home working a couple days a week and on the other days he was able to take Derek to school and work in the office. We all had to adjust. Each one of us has our own story from that time, our own perceptions and struggles, and our own blessings. We all experienced it differently, and we all had hope ripped from our hands on many occasions as more and more was taken from us, as the timeline got extended, and when it seemed we would never reach an end.

I don't know if things will ever be "normal" again. I compare it to the 9/11 tragedy, where there was life as we knew it before 9/11/2001 and life after that day. We now live in a post-pandemic society. There was a heaviness that landed on my heart. It was like our baseline stress levels were now taken up a few notches. I am forever grateful for my recovery community and that I made it my job to work with women walking the path of sober living. They were a lifeline I didn't even know I needed. Being able to show up daily for them and with them was the necessary medicine for me. No matter how long you live sober, the work never ends.

Thanksgiving and Christmas of 2020 were a welcome time of respite as we approached the end of what had seemed like 20 years all wrapped into one. Despite my ability to look relatively happy on the outside, to do the things that were expected of me, to work well with my clients and show up for my kids, inside there was a longing to heal. A desire to release the chains that were tightening around my heart and lungs, making it hard to breathe. I needed some time, some space to think and meditate and be with God in a way I never had before. I took the last two weeks of the year off, set some intentions for my time that included sleep, planning for my business, and the opportunity for quiet. I had no idea what was going to come of it, but I was open-minded. I made the decision to begin a formal meditation program, write daily, and practice morning mindfulness. My word of the year became "commit." As a result of selecting my word for the year, I committed to a few simple routines daily. Transforming our daily habits is a critical part of developing confidence beyond recovery. Sometimes we need a depth that can only come from the type of self-reflection I allowed during that break. What came out of it was a deep level of emotional understanding and healing. And nothing that is actually worth doing is easy. I was energized and felt stronger than ever about the direction of my life and the direction in which our family was going. The self-doubt that had been holding me back in my business was lifted, and the blessings of abundance started flowing my way.

CLOSING

THIS IS THE STORY OF MY LIFE. THE WORDS printed here are my perceptions and feelings felt over the last four decades. They are my truth. I have learned through years of self-discovery that included: a twelve-step program, therapy, acupuncture, prayer, coaching, and time. I have also learned that my story is my own and while others may see it differently, it's my own truth. I have experienced and grown a lot; I hope I never stop learning. I have loved hard. I am a deep feeler. I surrendered many years ago to God and chose to walk on a sober path.

There is very little I know for sure. Here is what I do know and have learned since the day I started this journey almost twenty years ago.

1. Addiction isn't a choice, but recovery is.
2. What happened to you isn't your fault, but healing is your responsibility.

3. In recovery, nothing changes if you don't change.
4. There is much love to give and receive in this world, and it's worth it.
5. Preparation is the key to success in life.
6. Just because I am sober doesn't mean I am well.
7. Most of the stories we tell ourselves are not true.
8. There is a God and I'm not Him (Thank God).
9. God and I are the only ones that can take care of me.
10. Nothing worth doing is easy.

My passion for sober women, and the recovery community in general, is deep and personal. It obviously comes from my own experience with addiction, but also from my time in twelve-step programs and clinical practice. Working with others in such an intimate setting as therapy changed me deeply. It opened the door to a whole new perspective on vulnerability, trauma, pain, and healing. I don't know that I would have believed some of the things people go through if I hadn't heard the horrific stories for myself. I wouldn't have understood the power of substances as much if I hadn't sat with women in both AA and in my clinical practice who were chronic relapsers and listened to their stories. I wouldn't have learned so much about what it really takes to build a life beyond recovery that we'll love and won't want to escape from. For most of us, this is the hardest thing we will ever do in life. After dealing with societal stigma, family isolation, loss of job opportunities, and negative thinking patterns, it feels impossible to imagine another way.

And I hope I find ways to keep sharing it, because now I know that's how it works. When we don't show up in this sober life as real people, with big feelings, vulnerable, raw, and exposed, others who are walking the path don't benefit. Shame is described as that feeling that I did something bad. And for recovering people, no doubt this is a prevalent and difficult emotion. Shame prevents people from being transparent, opening up to others, and from having deep and meaningful relationships. It's like a vine extending back for miles to years gone by that gets wrapped around your body over and over again, slowly tightening with every turn. It squeezes the very life out of you as you try to gasp for air in your present moment. The experience of feeling so alone in my life, even in recovery, and not hearing stories from other women who were like me tightened this hairy vine even more. The circulation was slowed to my brain. The overwhelm I felt in those years leading up to that tenth anniversary was a tsunami wave sucking back everything it covered. And I didn't even realize it. I knew that when I did go to AA meetings or spoke with the occasional authentic woman, others were doing it differently, they were more at peace.

This story isn't special or unique. It is personal to me but there are millions of others with similar paths who have been crippled by substance abuse, lost everything, and then rebuilt their lives. I know there are many ways to get sober. The modern addict has choices

I wouldn't have even been able to imagine when I first walked through the doors of rehab. Treatment facilities offer complementary medicine like ear acupuncture, drum therapy, and meditation practices. Essential oils are now used in treatment rooms and patients learn about nutrition and physical activity in relation to their mood. It is incredible watching this shift from traditional thinking into more contemporary and inclusive ways of working with substance abuse. Women who are getting sober have more resources than ever because of the internet. There are Facebook groups, sober coaches, online meetings, and recovery memberships. Recovery is more accessible than ever before. If you want it.

That's why I started a space for all women who want to grow and build confidence in recovery. An accessible Facebook group, Confident Sober Women, brings together like-minded women in a non-judgmental space without rules or dogma. Serving and supporting them has enhanced my recovery more than I could have imagined. Building content based on the knowledge I have of natural wellness and my clinical skills has been profound. I had no idea what was going to come of it when I started, and I wasn't sure it would work. I doubted that anyone would want what I had. The emotional roller coaster of entrepreneurship takes its toll, but every single day I remind myself that it's worth it. On the easy days, this is no problem. On the days I have cried during Zoom meetings, broken down in my bed at night with doubt, or as I lie in Epsom salt baths trying to soak the stress out, I remind myself that this work is important. If it helps one woman build a life she doesn't want to escape from, I am proud.

After the pandemic routine settled in, and left many people with trauma from job loss, relationship damages, mental health challenges for kids, and the triggering of past events, my private practice was overflowing with phone calls weekly. I have never had to turn people away before or carry a waiting list. Now, however, this appears to be the new normal. It hurts my heart to know I can't take them all. Even now two years after the start of the pandemic many people and families are suffering from the consequences of lockdown, school closures, loss of business, and an astronomical rise in substance abuse death.

I saw that women in recovery have a desire to devour good content which helps to elevate their lives beyond recovery. As a result, I created the Sober Freedom Inner Circle for sober women to be supported in their growth of emotional sobriety. What's amazing about the Inner Circle is that it provides the roadmap for moving away from fear and into confidence with accessibility to coaching from me plus other sober therapists. I still get shocked every time I ask another woman to donate her time and expertise to my program and she says "Yes". In fact, I have interacted with and built a very long list of women willing to contribute to our sober community in this way. I can't think of many other organizations where this is the case. Where people so willingly offer their time and talent in exchange for a handshake and a thank you. The recovery community is truly a special one. You can learn more about the Sober Freedom Inner Circle at www.shelbyjohncoaching.com/Innercircle.

When I look back now, I don't even recognize that pre-2002 woman I used to be. I can't even believe I am the same person. Making the decision to get and stay sober allowed me the opportunity to build a life worth living today. I am now able to show up in all the times, the good and the tragic alike. I can participate in my own life, even when I don't want to. The women in the beginning who were further along the path than I was gave me hope. The stories I heard were different from mine. This story is likely different from yours. while the situations are different, all of humanity can relate to the feelings. When I come alongside another woman struggling in recovery, I feel the desperation in her voice; I feel the defeat and despair. I relate to stories of shame and guilt due to her behavior during active addiction. We aren't all the same and that's actually a blessing. It's important to hear the journey of other addicts to solidify the fact that there is hope in recovery. Life never has to be that dark again. I have thoroughly enjoyed learning more about the modern substance abuser and their perception on the label of addict, their feelings about twelve-step programs, and their desire for education about how the brain and body function. This deepens the recovery experience for all and paves the way for folks who will meet us along the road for years to come.

There are numerous ways to get and stay sober, especially now. You have to find what works for you. There are people you aren't going to agree with along the way, who don't believe as you do or who do the re-covery process differently. Each person finds a way that builds the type of peace and serenity on the inside that accomplishes their goals. What matters is that you have a life you love beyond recovery. Abstinence is only the beginning; there is so much more to recovery than not using. It is the most beautiful and the most brutal life you could ever imagine. What I want you to know for sure is that if you have a longing for more, for deeper connections, for better health and more joy, it's out there for you. Winners stay consistent, they pursue growth, they don't make excuses, and they are real.

When you step into the sunlight of the Spirit, when you surrender to all the Universe has to offer you and the places where it comes into your life, the blessings of sobriety will rain down and flood your life. It is all available. You have to be your own biggest fan at all costs, make yourself a priority, and be willing to continue to recover in recovery.

Happiness and joy are not the same things. The word "happy" is fleeting, situational. It comes and goes depending on the circumstances. There have been many happy times in my sober life! So many golden moments with my children, with Ryan, with extended family and with friends. We laughed a lot. Derek cracks me up with his jokes and stories. It is fun watching each of our children grow into the person they are meant to be. We enjoy happy moments watching them participating in their activities, and learning information and skills for the first time. Teenagers are funny—they make us laugh all the time. Our times with extended family are cherished memories in my heart. Family vacations and holidays get re-lived over and over again as we talk at the family dinner table. Special traditions that we all look forward to have been cultivated over time. Our life has been incredibly blessed.

Joy is different. Joy is the brick and mortar of our lives, a lasting inside job. It's the place we arrive after years of practice, commitment, and sacrifice. True joy is when, despite all the craziness happening in life, even with all the heartbreak, grief, disappointment, anger, and sadness, you are solid on the inside. You have the kind of peace that tells you no matter what happens in your life, you are strong. Some parts of your life might not work out, but you will survive. The child might stay estranged, the husband might still leave, the job might be over, and you might not be healed, but on the inside, you know there is more than this momentary struggle. You can keep holding your torch to light the path. I don't know any person in recovery who can say they felt this while in active addiction. I don't know anyone that is living a life out of alignment with their personal core values who knows this serenity. I do know women who are putting one foot in front of the other despite the circumstances surrounding them. They are living despite their pain, and they have joy.

I strive to live that out on a daily basis. This is what I teach the women in my program and those who sit completely raw, vulnerable, and exposed on the couch in my office. In the beginning, it feels unrealistic. The women think that because they have anxiety, stress, and overwhelm, or because they have significant childhood trauma and unhealthy relationships, they can't improve their lives. As they work through their history, begin to take personal responsibility for their choices, and discover the tools necessary to live well in sobriety with joy, their eyes light up. They sit taller in their chair. You can tell their energy has changed, which then affects who and what is attracted to them. It is an incredible process. I get to witness miracles. Those miracles are why I keep coming back every day. This is why I get up in the morning, work through my own routine, take care of my family, and manage my emotions.

Change never stops. We see evidence of this in nature with the seasons, in our children as they grow from tiny humans into six feet tall thirteen-year-olds. We see it in the wrinkles and gray hairs that seem to multiply daily. The evolution of life never ends. Our family is changing. My daughters are growing into beautiful young women, beginning to connect with us in mature ways, and are seeing the possibilities for their futures. Looking back, I would never have imagined we could settle into a place of affection, kindness, mutual respect, and communication. Derek continues to be steady and stable. He is growing into a man-sized middle schooler, and he is handsome. His work ethic runs deep. He watches and works with his grandfathers to learn what they are willing to teach him. He is a competitive athlete with a deep love for God. It feels like he is an old soul, a deep thinker. Every time I see him, I am thankful that God sent me a son.

We have no idea what the future holds. None of us does. But the hope we have from being sober women and the hope that comes from God is better than any crystal ball. My goal in life is to be that light for as many people as I can, come alongside others to walk with them in the way they need, and never let them lose hope. I desire to show them, no matter where they are on their journey, there is always a way. The sun sets each day and then rises, and you get to try again.

Very Next Steps

THE SOBER FREEDOM TRANSFORMATION

If you felt a nudge in your heart as you were reading, a draw towards action, here is what you can do. Continue your work in recovery to build that emotional sobriety and confidence you long for. This is what is necessary to manage the emotions of real life. The truth that is happening all around you. The Sober Freedom Transformation is a 1:1 coaching program and does just that.

Learn more at
www.ShelbyJohnCoaching.com/Transformation.

Urgent Plea!

Thank You For Reading My Book!

I really appreciate all the feedback and love
hearing what you have to say.

I need your input to be sure I can make my
next book even better.

Please take two minutes to leave a review on Amazon
letting me know what you think of the book.

ABOUT THE AUTHOR

Shelby is a licensed clinical social worker with a private practice where she specializes in trauma, addictions, and anxiety. With years of experience in the field she founded Shelby John Coaching and is the happy host of the Confident Sober Women podcast. After getting sober, she became a fresh, authentic voice in the sobriety space showing women how to build confidence and love their lives beyond recovery. Shelby is a mother to three teenagers, a wife to one loving man, and obsessed with her furbabies.

CPSIA information can be obtained
at www.ICGtesting.com
Printed in the USA
BVHW071952120922
646805BV00011B/340